P9-DEZ-511

CONTENTS—ALPHABETICAL

IMPORTANT TELEPHONE NUMBERS
Area Codes: Manhattan & Bronx (212) — Bklyn, Queens, S.I. (718)

EMERGENCIES

Police	911	Dental Emergency	677-2510
Fire	911	Doctors on Call	(718) 238-2100
Ambulance	911	Drug Abuse	(800) 538-4840
To report a fire	628-2900	F. B. I.	553-2700
Fire Headquarters	(718) 403-1403	Gas/Steam/Electric	683-8830
Police Dept Info	374-5000	Heat Complaints	960-4800
Alcoholics Anonymous	473-6200	Highway	566-3406
Animal Bites	566-7105	Medical Help	(718) 326-0600
Arson Hotline	(718) 403-1300	Poison Control	764-7667
Battered Women	433-7297	Rape Hot Line	777-4000
Child Abuse	(800) 342-3720	Runaway Hotline	619-6884
Coast Guard	668-7936	Suicide Prevention	532-2400
Con Edison	683-8830	U.S. Secret Service	466-4400
Crime Victim Hotline	577-7777	Water/Sewer Emer	966-7500

RECORDED INFORMATION

Lottery Winning	976-2020	Racing (OTB)	976-2121
Metropolitan Museum	535-7710	Sky Information	769-5917
MOMA Film Program	708-9490	Sports	976-1313
Parking Info	566-4121	Stock Market	976-4141
Parks Events	360-1333	Subway/Bus	(718) 330-1234
Passport Info	541-7700	Time of Day	976-1616
Prayer	246-4200	Weather Forecast	976-1212

SERVICES

Air Pollution	966-7500	Mayor's Office	566-5700
Birth Control/Abortion	677-3320	Medicaid Information	594-3050
Boro President	669-8300	Medicare/Soc. Security	432-3232
Bus & Subway Info	330-1234	Planned Parenthood	541-7800
Chamber Commerce	561-2020	Port Authority-Kennedy	(718) 656-4444
Consumers Complaints	577-0111	Port Auth-La Guardia	(718) 476-5000
Convention Ctr (Javits)	216-2000	Potholes	566-2018
Day Care	334-7814	Roosevelt Island Tram	753-6626
Election Board (LWV)	674-8484	Sanitation	334-8590
Family Planning	677-3040	Senior Citizens	577-0800
Foreign Exchange	883-0400	Telegrams, Cables	962-7111
Health Department	285-9503	Towaways	971-0770
Housing Authority	306-3000	Train-To-Plane	(718) 858-7272
Income Tax (City)	306-5700	Transit Authority	330-1234
Income Tax (Federal)	732-0100	Travelers' Aid Society	944-0013
Income Tax (State)	(800) 342-3536	Unemployment Info	791-1400
Legal Aid Society	577-3300	Visitors/Convention Bur.	397-8200
Marriage Licenses	269-2900	Welfare Assistance	344-5241

NEW YORK WEATHER

Month	Average High	Average Low	Average Temperature	Average Humidity
January	38.5	25.9	32.2	64%
April	60.7	43.5	52.1	60%
July	85.2	68.0	76.6	67%
October	66.8	50.6	58.7	67%

Average annual rainfall: 42" — Average annual snowfall: 33.3"
Average wind speed: summer 10 mph; winter 15 mph
Growing season: 210 days — Sunshine: 60% of possible total
Temperature range: Extreme high 106° F. — Extreme low -15° F.

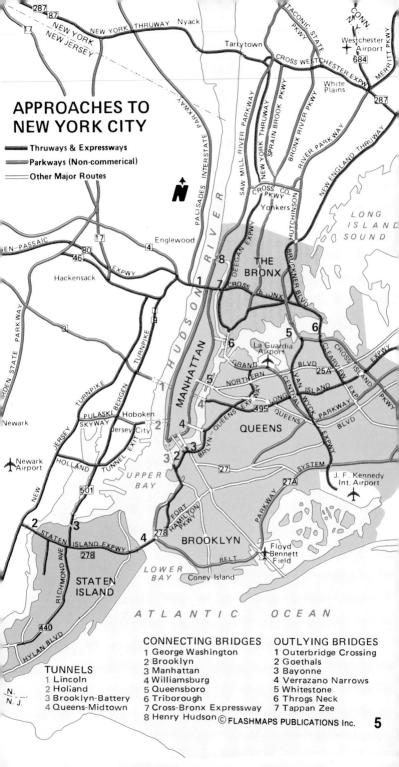

APPROACHES TO NEW YORK CITY

▬▬▬ Thruways & Expressways
▬▬ Parkways (Non-commerical)
▬ Other Major Routes

N

TUNNELS
1 Lincoln
2 Holland
3 Brooklyn-Battery
4 Queens-Midtown

CONNECTING BRIDGES
1 George Washington
2 Brooklyn
3 Manhattan
4 Williamsburg
5 Queensboro
6 Triborough
7 Cross-Bronx Expressway
8 Henry Hudson

OUTLYING BRIDGES
1 Outerbridge Crossing
2 Goethals
3 Bayonne
4 Verrazano Narrows
5 Whitestone
6 Throgs Neck
7 Tappan Zee

© FLASHMAPS PUBLICATIONS Inc.

5

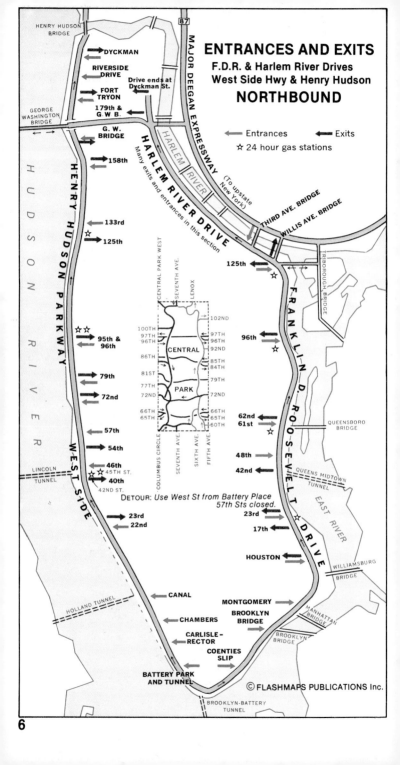

ENTRANCES AND EXITS
F.D.R. & Harlem River Drives
West Side Hwy & Henry Hudson
NORTHBOUND

← Entrances   ← Exits

☆ 24 hour gas stations

HENRY HUDSON BRIDGE

87

MAJOR DEEGAN EXPRESSWAY

HARLEM RIVER DRIVE

HARLEM RIVER

(To upstate New York)

Drive ends at Dyckman St.

Many exits and entrances in this section

DYCKMAN

RIVERSIDE DRIVE

FORT TRYON

179th & G.W.B.

G.W. BRIDGE

GEORGE WASHINGTON BRIDGE

158th

HUDSON RIVER

HENRY HUDSON PARKWAY

133rd

125th

THIRD AVE. BRIDGE

WILLIS AVE. BRIDGE

TRIBOROUGH BRIDGE

125th

FRANKLIN D. ROOSEVELT DRIVE

CENTRAL PARK WEST
SEVENTH AVE.
LENOX

100TH
97TH 96TH
86TH
81ST
77TH
72ND
66TH 65TH

102ND
97TH 96TH
92ND
85TH 84TH
79TH
72ND
66TH 65TH 60TH

CENTRAL PARK

COLUMBUS CIRCLE
SEVENTH AVE.
SIXTH AVE.
FIFTH AVE.

95th & 96th

79th

72nd

57th

54th

LINCOLN TUNNEL

46th
45TH ST.
40th
42ND ST.

WEST SIDE

96th

62nd
61st

48th

42nd

QUEENSBORO BRIDGE

QUEENS MIDTOWN TUNNEL

EAST RIVER

DETOUR: *Use West St from Battery Place 57th Sts closed.*

23rd
22nd

23rd

17th

HOUSTON

CANAL

HOLLAND TUNNEL

MONTGOMERY

BROOKLYN BRIDGE

CHAMBERS

CARLISLE-RECTOR

COENTIES SLIP

BATTERY PARK AND TUNNEL

WILLIAMSBURG BRIDGE

MANHATTAN BRIDGE

BROOKLYN BRIDGE

© FLASHMAPS PUBLICATIONS Inc.

BROOKLYN-BATTERY TUNNEL

6

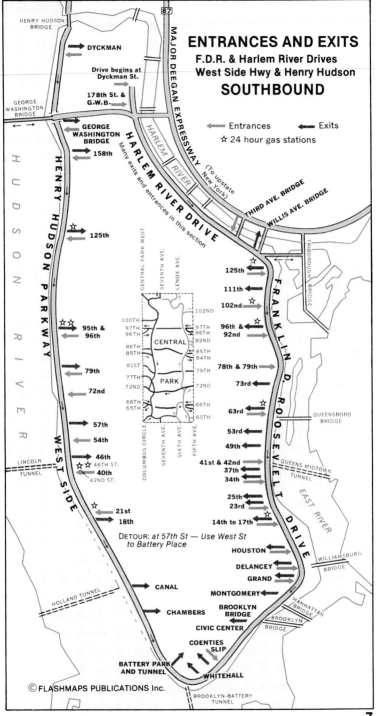

ENTRANCES AND EXITS
F.D.R. & Harlem River Drives
West Side Hwy & Henry Hudson
SOUTHBOUND

← Entrances   ← Exits
☆ 24 hour gas stations

HENRY HUDSON BRIDGE

DYCKMAN

Drive begins at Dyckman St.

178th St. & G.W.B.

MAJOR DEEGAN EXPRESSWAY

87

HARLEM RIVER

(To upstate New York)

GEORGE WASHINGTON BRIDGE

GEORGE WASHINGTON BRIDGE

158th

HARLEM RIVER DRIVE

Many exits and entrances in this section

THIRD AVE. BRIDGE

WILLIS AVE. BRIDGE

HUDSON RIVER

HENRY HUDSON PARKWAY

125th

☆ 95th & 96th

79th

72nd

57th

54th

46th
☆☆ 46TH ST.
40th
42ND ST.

WEST SIDE

☆ 21st
18th

LINCOLN TUNNEL

CENTRAL PARK WEST
SEVENTH AVE.
LENOX AVE.

100TH
97TH
96TH

86TH
85TH

81ST

77TH
72ND

66TH
65TH

CENTRAL PARK

102ND

97TH
96TH
92ND

85TH
84TH

79TH

72ND

66TH
60TH

COLUMBUS CIRCLE
SEVENTH AVE.
SIXTH AVE.
FIFTH AVE.

TRIBOROUGH BRIDGE

125th

111th

102nd ☆

96th & 92nd

78th & 79th

73rd

FRANKLIN D. ROOSEVELT DRIVE

QUEENSBORO BRIDGE

63rd ☆

53rd

49th

41st & 42nd

37th

34th

QUEENS MIDTOWN TUNNEL

25th

23rd ☆

14th to 17th

EAST RIVER

DETOUR: at 57th St — Use West St to Battery Place

HOUSTON

DELANCEY

GRAND

WILLIAMSBURG BRIDGE

CANAL

MONTGOMERY

HOLLAND TUNNEL

CHAMBERS

BROOKLYN BRIDGE

CIVIC CENTER

MANHATTAN BRIDGE

BROOKLYN BRIDGE

COENTIES SLIP

BATTERY PARK AND TUNNEL

WHITEHALL

© FLASHMAPS PUBLICATIONS Inc.

BROOKLYN-BATTERY TUNNEL

7

EAST-WEST SCALE OF MILES

To increase legibility all maps of Manhattan Island have been distorted in an east-west direction making two mileage scales necessary.

AVENUES AND
MAIN CROSS STREETS

░░ PLAZAS

THE BRONX

PLAZAS

Astor	3
Bowling Green	13
Chase Manhattan	11
Civic Center	7
Federal	6
Grand Army	2
Liberty	10
Lincoln Center	1
New York	14
Penn	5
Police	8
State Street	12
United Nations	4
World Trade	9

© FLASHMAPS PUBLICATIONS Inc.

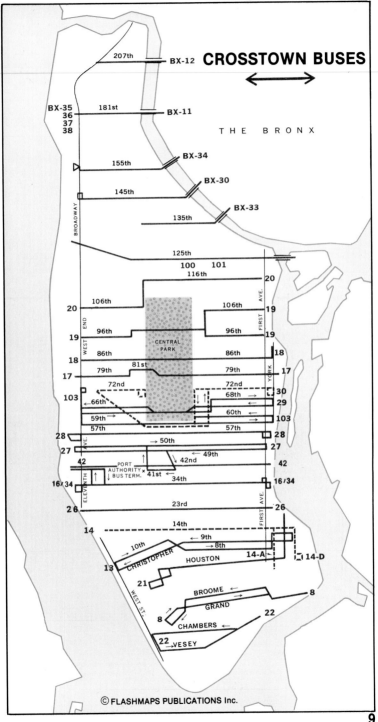

CROSSTOWN BUSES

THE BRONX

207th — BX-12

181st — BX-11

BX-35
36
37
38

155th — BX-34

145th — BX-30

135th — BX-33

125th

100   101

116th

20   106th   106th   19
20   19

BROADWAY

WEST END AVE.

FIRST AVE.

19   96th   96th   19

18   86th   86th   18

17   79th   81st   79th   17

72nd   72nd   30

103   29
    66th   68th   30
                  60th   103
    59th
    57th   57th

28   28
27   50th   27

    49th
42   42nd   42

PORT
AUTHORITY
BUS TERM.   41st

16/34   34th   16/34

ELEVENTH AVE.

26   23rd   26

14   14th   14

10th   9th
      8th
CHRISTOPHER   HOUSTON   14-A   14-D

13

WEST ST.

21

BROOME
GRAND   8
8
CHAMBERS   22
22   VESEY

© FLASHMAPS PUBLICATIONS Inc.

YORK AVE.

CENTRAL PARK

9

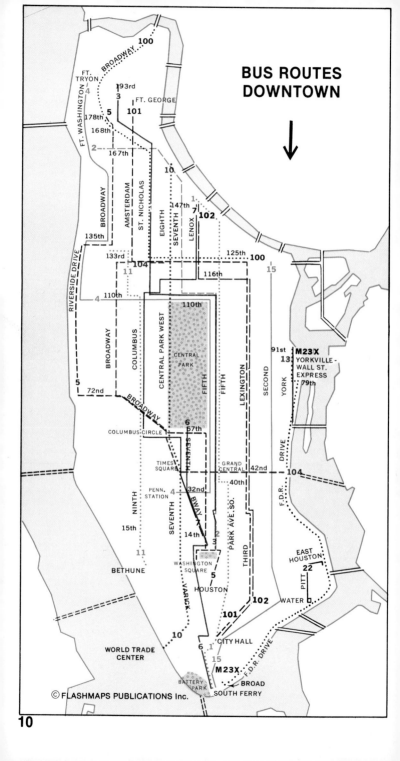

BUS ROUTES DOWNTOWN

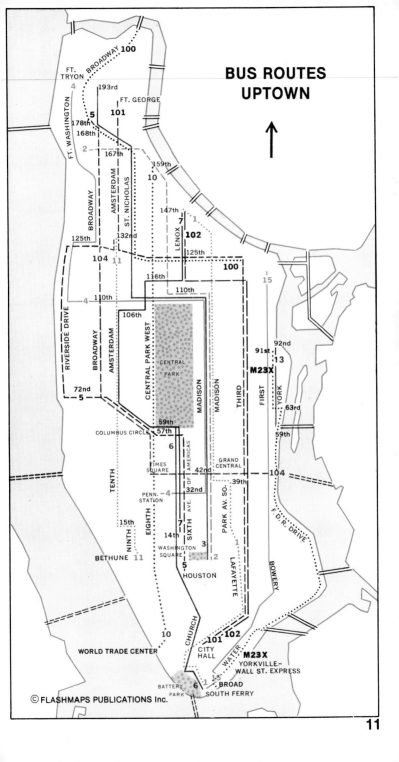

BUS ROUTES UPTOWN

© FLASHMAPS PUBLICATIONS Inc.

11

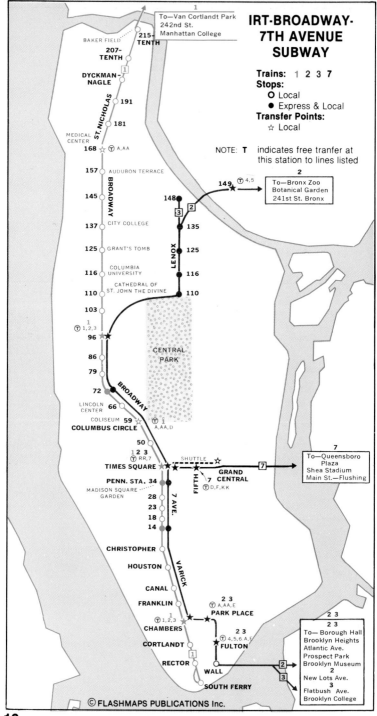

IRT-BROADWAY-7TH AVENUE SUBWAY

Trains: 1 2 3 7

Stops:
- O Local
- ● Express & Local

Transfer Points:
- ☆ Local

NOTE: **T** indicates free tranfer at this station to lines listed

To—Van Cortlandt Park
242nd St.
Manhattan College

215-TENTH
BAKER FIELD
207-TENTH
DYCKMAN-NAGLE
191
181
MEDICAL CENTER
168 T A, AA
157 AUDUBON TERRACE
145
137 CITY COLLEGE
125 GRANT'S TOMB
116 COLUMBIA UNIVERSITY
110 CATHEDRAL OF ST. JOHN THE DIVINE
103
96 T 1, 2, 3
86
79
72
66 LINCOLN CENTER
59 COLISEUM
COLUMBUS CIRCLE T A, AA, D

ST. NICHOLAS
BROADWAY

149 T 4,5
148
135 LENOX
125
116
110

To—Bronx Zoo
Botanical Garden
241st St. Bronx

CENTRAL PARK

50
TIMES SQUARE T 1 2 3 RR,7
PENN. STA. 34
MADISON SQUARE GARDEN
28
23
18
14
CHRISTOPHER
HOUSTON
CANAL
FRANKLIN
CHAMBERS T 1,2,3
CORTLANDT
RECTOR
SOUTH FERRY

7 AVE.
VARICK

SHUTTLE
GRAND CENTRAL
FIFTH
7 T D,F,KK

7

To—Queensboro Plaza
Shea Stadium
Main St.—Flushing

PARK PLACE 2 3 T A,AA,E
FULTON 2 3 T 4,5,6,A,E
WALL

2 3
2 3
To— Borough Hall
Brooklyn Heights
Atlantic Ave.
Prospect Park
Brooklyn Museum
2
New Lots Ave.
3
Flatbush Ave.
Brooklyn College

2
3

© FLASHMAPS PUBLICATIONS Inc.

12

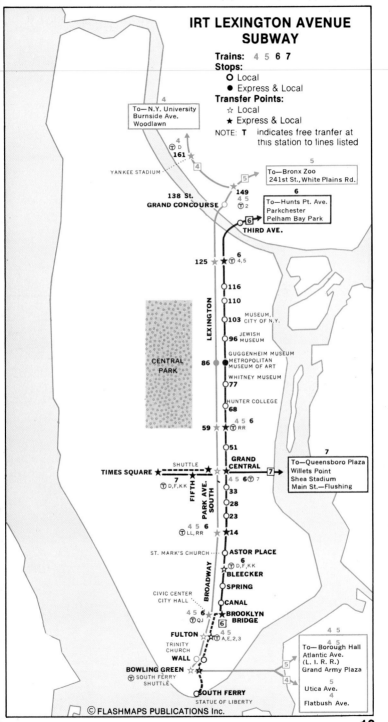

IRT LEXINGTON AVENUE SUBWAY

Trains: 4 5 **6 7**

Stops:
- ○ Local
- ● Express & Local

Transfer Points:
- ☆ Local
- ★ Express & Local

NOTE: **T** indicates free tranfer at this station to lines listed

To—N.Y. University
Burnside Ave.
Woodlawn

4
Ⓣ D
161 ★
YANKEE STADIUM ······· 4

5
To—Bronx Zoo
241st St., White Plains Rd.

149
4 5
Ⓣ 2

6
To—Hunts Pt. Ave.
Parkchester
Pelham Bay Park

138 St.
GRAND CONCOURSE

6
THIRD AVE.

125 ★★ 6
Ⓣ 4,5

116 ○
110 ○
103 ○   MUSEUM,
            CITY OF N.Y.
96 ●   JEWISH
           MUSEUM
           GUGGENHEIM MUSEUM
86 ●   METROPOLITAN
           MUSEUM OF ART
           WHITNEY MUSEUM
77 ○
           HUNTER COLLEGE
68 ○

59 ★★ 4 5 6
Ⓣ RR

51 ○
           GRAND CENTRAL

LEXINGTON

CENTRAL PARK

7
7
To—Queensboro Plaza
Willets Point
Shea Stadium
Main St.—Flushing

SHUTTLE
TIMES SQUARE ★ ☆ ☆
7   4 5 6 Ⓣ 7
Ⓣ D,F,KK

FIFTH   PARK AVE. SOUTH

33 ○
28 ○
23 ○
        4 5 6
        Ⓣ LL, RR
14 ★

ST. MARK'S CHURCH ······· **ASTOR PLACE** ○
                            6
                            Ⓣ D,F,KK
BLEECKER ○
SPRING ○
CIVIC CENTER
CITY HALL ······· **CANAL** ○
                   BROOKLYN
                   BRIDGE ●
                   4 5 6
                   Ⓣ QJ
6
FULTON ☆
TRINITY   4 5
CHURCH   Ⓣ A,E, 2,3
WALL ○
BOWLING GREEN ☆
Ⓣ SOUTH FERRY ★
SHUTTLE
SOUTH FERRY
STATUE OF LIBERTY

BROADWAY

4 5
4 5
To—Borough Hall
Atlantic Ave.
(L. I. R. R.)
Grand Army Plaza

5
Utica Ave.

5
Flatbush Ave.

© FLASHMAPS PUBLICATIONS Inc.

13

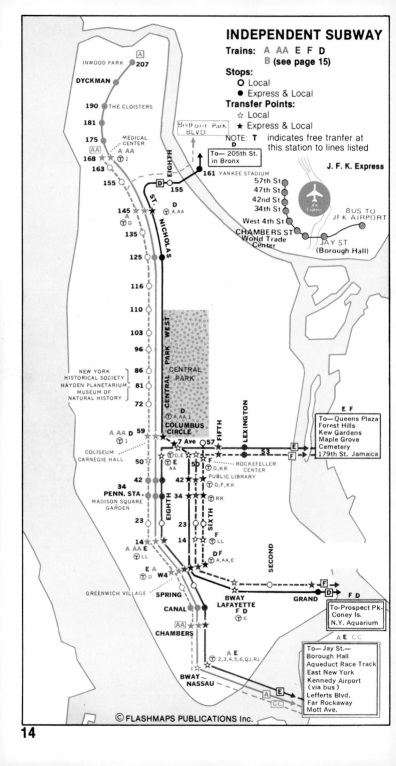

INDEPENDENT SUBWAY

Trains: A AA E F D
B **(see page 15)**

Stops:
○ Local
● Express & Local

Transfer Points:
☆ Local
★ Express & Local

NOTE: **T** indicates free tranfer at this station to lines listed

J. F. K. Express

57th St
47th St
42nd St
34th St
West 4th St
CHAMBERS ST
World Trade
Center

BUS TO
JFK AIRPORT

JAY St
(Borough Hall)

INWOOD PARK **A** **207**
DYCKMAN

190 THE CLOISTERS
181
175   MEDICAL
         CENTER
         A AA
AA
168   ★ T 1
163

155

145 ★ A AA
       T D
135   D A,AA

125

EIGHTH ST.
ST. NICHOLAS

D
155   D

161 YANKEE STADIUM

Bedford Park
BLVD
D
To— 205th St.
in Bronx

To— 205th St. in Bronx

116
110
103
96
86
81
72

NEW YORK
HISTORICAL SOCIETY
HAYDEN PLANETARIUM
MUSEUM OF
NATURAL HISTORY

CENTRAL PARK WEST

CENTRAL PARK

D
T A,AA,1

59 A AA D
    T 1
COLUMBUS
CIRCLE

COLISEUM
CARNEGIE HALL

50

42

34
PENN. STA.
MADISON SQUARE
GARDEN

23

14 A AA E
     T LL

E A
T D **W4**

GREENWICH VILLAGE

SPRING

CANAL

AA
CHAMBERS

7 Ave ○ **57**
★☆ T D,E
      E
     AA
5D F
     D,KK
     ROCKEFELLER
     CENTER
42 ★★ PUBLIC LIBRARY
        T D,F,KK
34 ★★ T RR
23 ○ ☆
       F
14 ☆ T LL
    D F
    T A,AA,E

FIFTH
LEXINGTON
EIGHTH
SIXTH
SECOND

E F
To— Queens Plaza
Forest Hills
Kew Gardens
Maple Grove
Cemetery
179th St. Jamaica

53 E
     F

BWAY
LAFAYETTE
F D
T 6

GRAND

F
D
F D

To-Prospect Pk-
Coney Is.
N.Y. Aquarium

A E
T 2,3,4,5,6,QJ,RJ

A E CC

BWAY
NASSAU

A **E**
   CC

To—Jay St.—
Borough Hall
Aqueduct Race Track
East New York
Kennedy Airport
(via bus)
Lefferts Blvd.
Far Rockaway
Mott Ave.

© FLASHMAPS PUBLICATIONS Inc.

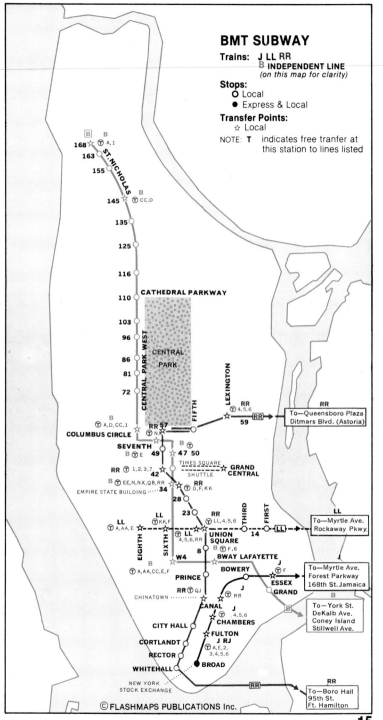

BMT SUBWAY

Trains: J LL RR
B INDEPENDENT LINE
(on this map for clarity)

Stops:
○ Local
● Express & Local

Transfer Points:
☆ Local

NOTE: **T** indicates free tranfer at this station to lines listed

B B
168 ☆ Ⓣ A, 1
163
155
ST. NICHOLAS
145 ☆ Ⓣ CC,D B
135
125
116
110 CATHEDRAL PARKWAY
103
96
86
81 CENTRAL PARK
72

CENTRAL PARK WEST

LEXINGTON

RR
☆ Ⓣ 4,5,6 RR
59 RR

To—Queensboro Plaza
Ditmars Blvd. (Astoria)

RR 57
COLUMBUS CIRCLE ☆ N
SEVENTH FIFTH
B Ⓣ E
47 50
49
RR Ⓣ 1,2,3,7 42 ☆
B Ⓣ EE,N,NX,QB,RR 34
EMPIRE STATE BUILDING 28
23

TIMES SQUARE
SHUTTLE
GRAND
CENTRAL

Ⓣ D,F,KK

LL
Ⓣ KK,F
SIXTH
EIGHTH
LL
Ⓣ A,AA,E

RR
Ⓣ LL,4,5,6
LL
Ⓣ 4,5,6,RR
UNION
SQUARE
THIRD FIRST
14 LL
To—Myrtle Ave.
Rockaway Pkwy.

W4 8
B Ⓣ F,6
BWAY LAFAYETTE
B
Ⓣ A,AA,CC,E,F
BOWERY
J
Ⓣ F
ESSEX
GRAND
To—Myrtle Ave.
Forest Parkway
168th St.Jamaica

PRINCE
RR Ⓣ QJ
CHINATOWN
J
Ⓣ RR
B
To—York St.
DeKalb Ave.
Coney Island
Stillwell Ave.

CANAL
J
,4,5,6
CHAMBERS
CITY HALL
FULTON
J RJ
Ⓣ A,E,2,
3,4,5,6
CORTLANDT
RECTOR
WHITEHALL ● BROAD
NEW YORK
STOCK EXCHANGE
RR
To—Boro Hall
95th St.
Ft. Hamilton

© FLASHMAPS PUBLICATIONS Inc.

MIDTOWN HOTELS

Streets (west side, top to bottom): W. 74th, W. 73rd, W. 72nd, W. 71st, W. 70th, W. 69th, W. 68th, W. 67th, W. 66th, W. 65th, W. 64th, W. 63rd, W. 62nd, W. 61st, W. 60th, W. 59th, W. 58th, W. 57th, W. 56th, W. 55th, W. 54th, W. 53rd, W. 52nd, W. 51st, W. 50th, W. 49th, W. 48th, W. 47th, W. 46th, W. 45th, W. 44th, W. 43rd, W. 42nd, W. 41st, W. 40th, W. 39th, W. 38th, W. 36th, W. 35th, W. 34th, W. 33rd, W. 32nd, W. 31st, W. 30th, W. 29th, W. 28th, W. 27th, W. 26th, W. 24th, W. 23rd, W. 22nd, W. 21st

Streets (east side, top to bottom): E. 77th, E. 76th, E. 75th, E. 70th, E. 69th, E. 68th, E. 67th, E. 66th, E. 65th, E. 64th, E. 63rd, E. 62nd, E. 61st, E. 60th, E. 59th, E. 58th, E. 57th, E. 56th, E. 55th, E. 54th, E. 53rd, E. 52nd, E. 51st, E. 50th, E. 49th, E. 48th, E. 47th, E. 46th, E. 45th, E. 44th, E. 43rd, E. 42nd, E. 41st, E. 40th, E. 39th, E. 38th, E. 37th, E. 36th, E. 35th, E. 34th, E. 33rd, E. 32nd, E. 31st, E. 30th, E. 29th, E. 28th, E. 27th, E. 26th, E. 25th, E. 24th, E. 23rd, E. 22nd, E. 21st

Avenues (west): ELEVENTH AVENUE, TENTH AVENUE, NINTH AVENUE, EIGHTH AVENUE, SEVENTH AVENUE, AVENUE OF THE AMERICAS, WEST END AVENUE, AMSTERDAM AVENUE, COLUMBUS AVENUE, BROADWAY, CENTRAL PARK WEST, (SIXTH AVENUE)

Avenues (east): FIFTH AVENUE, MADISON AVENUE, PARK AVE., LEXINGTON AVENUE, THIRD AVENUE, SECOND AVENUE, FIRST AVENUE

Landmarks: CENTRAL PARK, CENT. PK. SO., COLUMBUS CIRCLE, TIMES SQUARE, BRYANT PARK, VANDERBILT, GRAND CENTRAL, PENN STATION, MADISON SQUARE GARDEN, JACOB JAVITS CONVENTION CENTER, MADISON SQUARE PARK, GR. PK. N., GRAMERCY PARK, UNITED NATIONS

©FLASHMAPS PUBLICATIONS Inc.

16

MIDTOWN HOTELS—BY MAP NUMBERS

1 Madison Ave	33 Gorham	63 Helmsley Middlet'wn
2 Carlyle	34 Warwick	64 YMCA Vanderbilt
3 Surrey	35 Maxim's de Paris	65 Century Paramount
4 Westbury	36 St. Regis	66 Marriott Marquis
5 Mayfair Regent	37 Elysee	67 Milford Plaza
6 Plaza Athenee	38 Howard Hotel	68 Times Square
7 Lyden Gardens	39 New York Hilton	69 Travel Inn
8 YMCA West Side	40 Dorset	70 Wentworth
9 Empire	41 Howard Johnson	71 Roosevelt
10 Mayflower	42 Novotel	72 Algonquin
11 Lowell, The	43 Sheraton City Squire	75 Grand Hyatt
12 Golden Tulip	44 Sheraton Centre	76 UN Plaza/Tower
13 Regency, The	44 Sheraton Tower	77 Helmsley New York
14 Pierre Hotel	45 Omni Bershire	78 Tudor
15 Sherry Netherlands	46 Lyden House	79 Bedford
16 Essex House	47 Grand Bay	80 Doral Park Ave
17 Ritz Carlton	48 Helmsley Palace	81 Doral Court
18 St Moritz	49 Loew's Summit	81 Doral Tuscany
19 Park Lane Helmsley	49 San Carlos	82 Eastgate
20 Plaza, Westin	50 Beverly	83 Morgan's
21 Westpark	51 Plaza 50	84 Madison Towers
22 Days Inn	52 Best West Skyline	85 Kitano
23 Parker Meridien	53 Waldorf-Astoria	86 Sheraton Park Ave
24 Salisbury	54 Halloran House	87 Shelburne Murray Hill
25 Helmsley Windsor	55 Doral Inn	88 Comfort Inn
26 Wyndham	56 Beekman Tower	89 YMCA Sloane Hse
27 Blackstone	57 Ramada Inn	90 Dumont Plaza
28 Shoreham	58 Consulate	91 New York Penta
29 Drake Swissotel	59 Edison	92 Southgate Tower
30 Lombardy	60 Inter-Continental NY	93 Palace International
31 Omni Park Central	61 Lexington	94 YMCA McBurney
32 Wellington	62 Roger Smith Winthrp	95 Gramercy Park

MIDTOWN HOTELS—ALPHABETICAL

Hotel/Motel (Room Rate) ★	Address	Map No	Telephone	Rooms
Algonquin (b)	59 W 44th	72	840-6800	200
Bedford (c)	118 E 40th	79	697-4800	200
Beekman Tower (b)	3 Mitchell Place	56	355-7300	160
Best West Skyline (c)	Tenth Ave & 50th	52	586-3400	240
Beverly (c)	125 E 50th	50	753-2700	300
Blackstone (c)	50 E 58th	27	355-4200	183
Carlyle (a)	35 E 76th	2	744-1600	180
Century Paramount (c)	235 W 46th	65	764-5500	650
Comfort Inn (c)	42 W 35th Street	88	947-0200	132
Consulate Hotel (c)	224 W 49th Street	58	246-5252	295
Days Inn (c)	440 W 57th	22	581-8100	588
Doral Court (a)	130 E 39th	81	685-1100	220
Doral Inn (c)	541 Lexington at 49th	55	755-1200	700
Doral Park Avenue (b)	70 Park Ave	80	687-7050	200
Doral Tuscany (a)	120 E 39th	81	686-1600	200
Dorset (b)	30 W 54th	40	247-7300	150
Drake Swissotel (a)	440 Park Ave	29	421-0900	650
Dumont Plaza (b)	E 34th betw 3rd & Lex	90	481-7600	257
Eastgate (b)	222 E 39th	82	687-8000	192

★ ROOM RATES (DOUBLE): (a) $200-270 (b) $150-200 (c) $90-150 **17**

Hotel/Motel (Room Rate) ★	Address	Map No	Telephone	Rooms
Edison (c)	228 W 47th	59	840-5000	1000
Elysee Hotel (b)	60 E 54th St	37	753-1066	110
Empire (c)	Broadway & 63rd	9	265-7400	500
Essex House (a)	160 Central Park S	16	247-0300	700
Golden Tulip Barbizon (b)	140 E 63rd	12	838-5700	340
Gorham (c)	136 W 55th	33	245-1800	170
Gramercy Park (c)	Lexington & 21st	95	475-4320	500
Grand Bay (a)	152 W 51st Street	47	765-1900	178
Grand Hyatt New York (a)	Lexington & 42nd St	75	883-1234	1407
Halloran House (b)	525 Lexington	54	755-4000	650
Helmsley Middletown (b)	148 E 48th	63	755-3000	245
Helmsley New York (a)	212 E 42nd St	77	490-8900	800
Helmsley Palace (a+)	455 Madison Ave	48	888-7000	1050
Helmsley Windsor (b)	100 W 58th Street	25	265-2100	300
Howard Hotel (a+)	127 E 55th Street	38	826-1100	107
Howard Johnson (c)	Eighth Ave & W 52nd	41	581-4100	300
Inter-Continental NY (a)	111 E 48th	60	755-5900	680
Kitano (c)	66 Park Avenue	85	685-0022	90
Lexington (b)	Lexington & 48th	61	755-4400	800
Loews Summit (b)	Lexington & 51st	49	752-7000	760
Lombardy (b)	111 E 56th	30	753-8600	330
Lowell, The (a)	28 East 63rd St	11	838-1400	60
Lyden Gardens (b)	215 E 64th St	7	355-1230	133
Lyden House (b)	320 E 53rd St	46	888-6070	81
Madison Avenue (b)	25 E 77th Street	1	744-4300	284
Madison Towers (b)	22 E 38th	84	685-3700	250
Marriott Marquis (a)	1535 Broadway	66	398-1900	1879
Maxim's de Paris (a+)	700 Fifth Ave	35	247-2200	250
Mayfair Regent (a)	Park Ave & 65th	5	288-0800	199
Mayflower (b)	15 Central Park West	10	265-0060	575
Milford Plaza (c)	270 W 45th	67	869-3600	1310
Morgan's (b)	237 Madison Avenue	83	686-0300	115
New York Hilton (a)	1335 Ave of Amer	39	586-7000	2131
New York Penta (b)	401 Seventh Ave & 33rd	91	736-5000	1705
Novotel (b)	226 W 52nd	42	315-0100	470
Omni Berkshire Place (a)	21 E 52nd	45	753-5800	415
Omni Park Central (b)	Seventh Ave & 55th	31	247-8000	1400
Palace International (c)	429 Park Ave South	93	532-4860	60
Park Lane Helmsley (a)	36 Central Park S	19	371-4000	640
Parker Meridien (a)	118 W 55th	23	245-5000	700
Pierre (a+)	Fifth Ave & 61st	14	838-8000	195
Plaza Athenee (a+)	37 E 64th Street	6	734-9100	170
Plaza 50 (b)	155 E 50th Street	51	751-5710	206
Plaza Westin (a+)	Fifth Ave & 59th	20	759-3000	1000
Ramada Inn (c)	Eighth Ave & 48th	57	581-7000	363
Regency (a)	Park Ave & 61st	13	759-4100	400
Ritz Carlton (a)	112 Central Park South	17	757-1900	250
Roger Smith Winthrop (c)	501 Lexington	62	755-1400	180
Roosevelt (b)	45 E 45th	71	661-9600	1080
St. Moritz (a)	50 Central Park S	18	755-5800	772
St. Regis (Sheraton) (a+)	Fifth Ave & 55th	36	753-4500	525

MIDTOWN HOTELS—ALPHABETICAL (Continued)

Hotel/Motel (Room Rate) ★	Address	Map No	Telephone	Rooms
Salisbury (c)	123 W 57th	**24**	246-1300	320
San Carlos (c)	150 E 50th St	**49**	755-1800	200
Shelburne Murray Hill (b)	303 Lexington Avenue	**87**	689-5200	248
Sheraton Centre (b +)	811 Seventh Ave & 52nd	**44**	581-1000	1850
Sheraton City Squire (b)	Seventh Ave at 52nd St	**43**	581-3300	720
Sheraton Park Ave (c)	45 Park Ave at 37th	**86**	685-7676	160
Sheraton Towers (a)	Seventh Ave at 52nd St	**44**	581-1000	151
Sherry Netherland (a)	781 Fifth Ave	**15**	355-2800	200
Shoreham (c)	33 W 55th Street	**28**	247-6700	150
Southgate Tower (c)	Seventh Ave & 31st	**92**	563-1800	520
Stanhope (a + +)	Fifth Ave & 81st St	off map	288-5800	270
Surrey, The (b)	20 E 76th Street	**3**	288-3700	113
Times Square Motor (c-)	Eighth Ave & 43rd	**68**	354-7900	720
Travel Inn (c)	515 W 42nd	**69**	695-7171	160
Tudor (c)	304 E 42nd	**78**	986-8800	500
United Nations Plaza (a)	1 UN Plaza	**76**	355-3400	288
United Nations Tower (a)	2 UN Plaza	**76**	355-3400	115
Vista International (a)	3 World Trade Ctr	off map	938-9100	825
Waldorf-Astoria (a)	301 Park Ave	**53**	355-3000	2000
Warwick (b)	65 W 54th	**34**	247-2700	500
Wellington (c)	Seventh Ave & 55th	**32**	247-3900	700
Wentworth (c)	59 W 46th	**70**	719-2300	250
Westbury (a)	Madison Ave at 69th	**4**	535-2000	300
Westpark Hotel (c)	308 W 58th	**21**	246-6440	80
Wyndham (c)	42 W 58th Street	**26**	753-3500	200
YMCA McBurney (c-)	215 W 23rd	**94**	741-9226	279
YMCA Sloane House (c-)	356 W 34th	**89**	760-5850	1492
YMCA Vanderbilt (c-)	224 E 47th	**64**	755-2410	430
YMCA West Side (c-)	5 W 63rd	**8**	787-4400	700

★ ROOM RATES (DOUBLE): (a) $200-270   (b) $150-200   (c) $90-150

PARKING INFORMATION

Parking Area	Address	Capacity	Hourly Rate
Municipal Parking	Eighth Ave & 53rd	450	$ .85 (½ hr)
Municipal Lot	Leonard St & Lafayette	150	1.00 (1 hr)
Municipal Parking	Delancey & Essex	361	.30 (½ hr)
Municipal Parking	Park Row & Pearl	402	1.00 (½ hr)

There are about 900 private parking garages in Manhattan.
Minimum $8.50 to $11.50 (first hour); maximum $12.00 to $35.00 (10 to 12 hours).

PARKING VIOLATIONS

No-parking zone: Manhattan, 23rd St to 72nd St, river to river,
   except where metered. (Fine for expired meter $40.00)
All parking tickets: $40.00   Double Parking: $35 to $40   Hydrants: $40
Cars towed-away: $75 plus $40 summons. Car will be found under the
   West Side Hwy at 36th St (Tel: 349-7028). Storage charge per day $5.
Alternate parking: One side Mon/Wed/Fri; **Other side** Tues/Thur/Sat;
   See street signs.
Sundays & Holidays: Most street parking regulations suspended.
Traffic Tickets: 770 Broadway   **Telephone:** 477-4430.

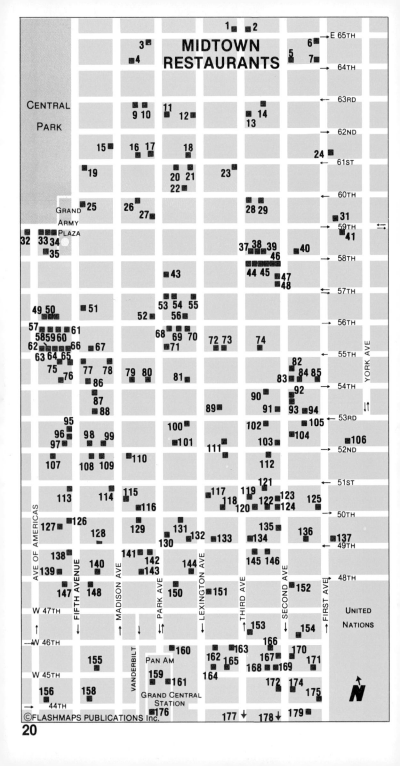

MIDTOWN RESTAURANTS

CENTRAL PARK

GRAND ARMY PLAZA

GRAND CENTRAL STATION

PAN AM

UNITED NATIONS

YORK AVE

AVE OF AMERICAS

FIFTH AVENUE

MADISON AVE

VANDERBILT

PARK AVE

LEXINGTON AVE

THIRD AVE

SECOND AVE

FIRST AVE

E 65TH
64TH
63RD
62ND
61ST
60TH
59TH
58TH
57TH
56TH
55TH
54TH
53RD
52ND
51ST
50TH
49TH
48TH
W 47TH
W 46TH
W 45TH
W 44TH

© FLASHMAPS PUBLICATIONS Inc.

MIDTOWN RESTAURANTS—BY MAP NUMBERS

1 Sign of the Dove	49 Il Gattopardo	93 La Mangeoire
2 David K's	50 Abruzzi	94 Louise Jr
3 Le Cirque	50 Aperitivo	95 Top of the Sixes
4 Le Regence	51 Terrace	96 Stouffer's
5 Primola	52 Lafayette	97 Twenty-One Club
6 Auntie Yuan	53 Mitsukoshi	98 La Grenouille
7 Maxwell's Plum	54 Bruce Ho's	99 La Galerie
9 Orsini's	55 Le Chantilly	99 Rendez-Vous
10 Post House, The	56 Laurent	100 Brasserie
11 Huberts	57 Cafe de Nice	101 Four Seasons
12 Demarchelier	58 Romeo Salta	102 Tang's Chariot
13 La Cour St Germain	59 Miyako	103 Argenteuil, Cafe
14 Bravo Gianni	60 Kurumazushi	103 Peccavi
15 L'Omnibus Maxim's	61 Il Tinello	104 Eamonn Doran
15 Maxim's	62 Cafe Geneva	105 Zapata
16 Madame Romaine	63 French Shack	106 Le Perigord
17 Capriccio	64 L'Escargot	107 San Marco
18 Il Valletto	64 La Fondue	108 Il Menestrello
19 Pierre Hotel Cafe	65 Adrienne	109 Bombay Palace
20 Le Festival	65 Le Bistro d'Adrienne	110 Scarlatti's
21 Jacqueline's	66 La Caravelle	111 Beijing Duckhouse
22 Le Veau d'Or	67 La Cote Basque	111 Nippon
23 Isle of Capri	68 Le Manoir	112 L'Endroit
24 Cine Citta	69 Benihana of Tokyo	113 Assembly
25 Quaglino's	70 Doriental	114 Tse Yang
26 Pronto	71 PJ Clarke's	115 Le Trianon
27 Regine	72 Shun Lee Palace	116 Goucester House
28 Yellowfinger	73 Enoteca Iperbole	117 Kenny's Steak
29 Arizona 206	74 Michael's Pub	118 La Table des Rois
31 Brive	75 Acquavit	118 Nada Sushi
32 Cafe de la Paix	75 Italian Pavilion	119 Le Bistro
32 Jockey Club	76 Raphael	120 Carpaccio
33 Mickey Mantle's	77 King Cole	121 Torremolinos
33 Nirvana	78 Quilted Giraffe	122 Lutece
33 Park Room	79 Le Cygne	123 La Mediterranee
34 Edwardian Room	80 Lello	124 Leopard
34 Oak Room	81 Weston's	125 Wylie's Ribs
35 Manhattan Ocean	82 Elmer's	126 American Festival
37 Gian Marino	83 El Morocco	126 Sea Grill
37 La Camelia	84 Cafe Europa	127 Rainbow Room
38 Tino's	85 India Pavilion	128 Sushiden
39 Felidia	86 Bice	129 Giambelli
40 Cafe Nicholson	87 Prunelle	130 Waldorf Peacock
41 Sandro's	88 Seryna	131 Gin-Ray of Japan
43 Akbar	89 Alfredo	132 Bull & Bear
44 Dawat	89 Auberge Suisse	132 Inagiku
44 Dewey Wong	89 Avgerinos	133 Christo's
44 Girafe	89 Charley O's	134 Smith & Wolensky
45 Anche Vivolo	89 Les Tournebroches	134 Tonino
45 Tre Scalini	89 Nyborg & Nelson	135 San Giusto
46 Bruno	89 Oscar's	136 Antolotti's
46 Cafe 58	90 Toscana	137 Coq d'Or
47 Le Steak	91 Il Nido	138 La Reserve
48 Les Sans-Culottes	92 Chez Louis	139 Charley O's

140 Hatsuhana	153 Joe & Rose	168 Pen & Pencil
141 Tandoor	154 Awoki	169 John Barleycorn
142 Aurora	155 Cattleman	170 Captain's Table
143 Shinbashi	156 Algonquin	170 Flower Drum
144 Barclay's	158 Sagano	171 L'Incontro
145 Chin Chin	159 Takesushi	172 Palm
146 Box Tree	160 Trattoria	174 Palm Too
146 Darjeeling	161 Charlie Brown's	175 Ambassador Grill
147 Pearl's Chinese	162 Nanni	176 Oyster Bar
148 Chalet Suisse	163 Christ Cella	177 Crystal Fountain
150 Jsung Dynasty	164 Press Box	177 Pietro's
150 Menage a Trois	165 Le Cheval Blanc	177 Trumpet's
151 Nibbles	166 Spark's Steak	178 La Bibliotheque
152 Il Bambino d'Oro	167 Chef Chan	179 Sichuan Pavilion

MIDTOWN RESTAURANTS—ALPHABETICAL

Restaurant	Address	Map No.	Cuisine	Average Price ★	Telephone
Abruzzi	37 W 56th St	50	Continental	$19.50	489-8110
Acquavit	13 W 54th St	75	Scndinavin	45.00	307-7311
Adrienne	Maxim's Hotel	65	French	70 +	247-2200
Akbar	475 Park Ave	43	Indian	20-30	838-1717
Alfredo	Citicorp Center	89	Italian	15-25	371-3367
Algonquin	59 W 44th St	156	Amer/Contl	20-35	840-6800
Ambassador Grill	UN Plaza Hotel	175	Fr/Contl	25-30	702-5014
American Festival	Rockefeller Ctr	126	American	23-25	246-6699
Anche Vivolo	222 E 58th St	45	Italian	25-30	308-0112
Antolotti's	337 E 49th St	136	N. Italian	18-25	688-6767
Aperitivo	29 W 56th St	50	Italian	25-35	765-5155
Argenteuil, Cafe	253 E 52nd St	103	Internatl	38-40	753-9273
Arizona 206	206 E 60th St	29	S. Western	25-30	838-0440
Assembly, The	16 W 51st St	113	Steak/Sfd	30-45	581-3580
Auberge Suisse	Citicorp Center	89	Swiss	15-30	421-1420
Auntie Yuan	1191 A First Ave	6	Chinese	25-35	744-4040
Aurora	60 E 49th St	142	French	50 +	692-9292
Avgerinos	Citicorp Center	89	Greek	15-20	688-8828
Awoki	305 E 46th St	154	Japanese	20-35	759-8897
Barclay's	Intercontl Hotel	144	American	55-60	421-4389
Beijing Duckhouse	144 E 52nd St	111	Chinese	15-25	759-8260
Benihana of Tokyo	120 E 56th St	69	Japanese	20-25	593-1627
Bice	7 E 54th St	86	N. Italian	35-40	688-1999
Bombay Palace	30 W 52nd St	109	Indian	15-25	541-7777
Box Tree, The	250 E 49th St	146	Continental	58.00	758-8320
Brasserie	100 E 53rd St	100	French	20-25	751-4840
Bravo Gianni	230 E 63rd St	14	Italian	30-35	752-7272
Brive	405 E 58th St	31	Fr/Contl	50 +	838-9393
Bruce Ho's Four Seas	116 E 57th St	54	Chinese	12-16	753-2610
Bruno	240 E 58th St	46	N. Italian	25-35	688-4190
Bull & Bear	Lex & 49th St	132	American	20-30	872-4900
Cafe de la Paix	50 Central Pk S	32	Continental	45 +	755-5800
Cafe de Nice	56 W 56th St	57	Fr/Ital	17-21	586-7812
Cafe Europa	347 E 54th St	84	Modern Fr	15-25	755-0160
Cafe 58	232 E 58th St	46	French	20-25	758-5665
Cafe Geneva	69 W 55th St	62	Italian	20-33	489-7655
Cafe Nicholson	323 E 58th St	40	Continental	40-45	355-6769
Capriccio	33 E 61st St	17	No. Italian	35-40	757-7795
Captain's Table	860 Second Ave	170	Seafood	45-50	697-9538

22

★ Prices do not include drinks or gratuities

MIDTOWN RESTAURANTS Continued

Restaurant	Address	Map No.	Cuisine	Average Price ★	Telephone
Carpaccio	227 E 50th St	120	N. Italian	$25-30	838-7808
Cattleman	5 E 45th St	155	Steak/Sfd	20-30	661-1200
Chalet Suisse	6 E 48th St	148	Swiss	35-45	355-0855
Charley O's	33 W 48th St	139	Irish/Amer	15-20	582-7141
Charley O's	Citicorp Center	89	Irish/Amer	15-20	752-2102
Charlie Brown's	Pan Am Bldg	161	Steak/Sfd	15-25	661-2520
Chef Chan	845 Second Ave	167	Chinese	15-20	647-7471
Chez Louis	1016 Second Av	92	French	35-45	752-1400
Chin Chin	216 E 49th St	145	Chinese	25-35	888-4555
Christ Cella	160 E 46th St	163	Steak	55+	697-2479
Christo's	143 E 49th St	143	Stk/Contl	25-35	355-2695
Cine Citta	1134 First Ave	24	Italian	40-45	486-6226
Coq d'Or	5 Mitchell Place	137	French	40-45	826-1084
Crystal Fountain	Grand Hyatt Hotel	177	Continental	55+	850-5998
Darjeeling	248 E 49th	146	Indian	10-20	355-1810
David K's	1115 Third Ave	2	Chinese	30-35	371-9090
Dawat	210 E 58th St	44	Indian	20-30	355-7555
Demarchelier	808 Lexington	12	French	30-35	223-0047
Dewey Wong	206 E 58th St	44	Chinese	25-30	758-6881
Doriental	128 E 56th St	70	Chinese	15-25	688-8070
Eamonn Doran	998 Second Ave	104	Continental	20-25	752-8088
Edwardian Room	Plaza Hotel	34	Continental	50+	546-5310
El Morocco	307 E 54th	83	Continental	50+	750-1500
Elmer's	1034 Second Ave	82	Steak/Sfd	35-40	751-8020
Enoteca Iperbole	137 E 55th St	73	Italian	20-30	759-9720
Felidia	243 E 58th St	39	No. Italian	45-50	758-1479
Flower Drum	856 Second Ave	170	Chinese	12-25	697-4280
Four Seasons	99 E 52nd St	101	Continental	60-100	754-9494
French Shack	65 W 55th St	63	French	15-25	246-5126
Giambelli 50th St	46 E 50th St	129	North Ital	50+	688-2760
Gian Marino	237 E 58th St	37	Italian	35-40	752-1696
Gin-Ray of Japan	148 E 50th St	131	Japanese	15-20	759-7454
Girafe	208 E 58th St	44	North Ital	45-55	752-3054
Gloucester House	37 E 50th St	116	Seafood	35-50	755-7394
Hatsuhana	17 E 48th St	140	Japanese	25-35	355-3345
Huberts	575 Park Ave	11	American	55.00	673-3711
Il Bambino d'Oro	890 Second Ave	152	Italian	20-25	308-5515
Il Gattopardo	49 W 56th St	49	Italian	35-40	586-3978
Il Menestrello	14 E 52nd St	108	N. Italian	40-45	421-7588
Il Nido	251 E 53rd St	91	Italian	40-50	753-8450
Il Tinello	16 W 56th	61	Italian	30-35	245-4388
Il Valletto	133 E 61st St	18	Italian	45-50	838-3939
Inagiku	111 E 49th St	132	Japanese	35-45	355-0440
India Pavilion	325 E 54th St	85	Indian	10-15	223-9740
Isle of Capri	1028 Third Ave	23	Italian	20-25	758-1828
Italian Pavilion	24 W 55th St	75	Italian	25-35	586-5950
Jacqueline's Chmpgne	132 E 61st St	21	Swiss Fr	32-38	838-4559
Jockey Club	Ritz Carlton	32	Continental	50+	664-7700
Joe & Rose	747 Third Ave	153	Italian/Stk	30-35	980-3985
John Barleycorn Pub	209 E 45th St	169	Irish/Amer	10-15	986-1088
Jsung Dynasty	Lexington Htl	150	Japanese	20-30	355-1200
Kenny's Steak Pub	565 Lexington Av	117	American	20-30	355-0666
King Cole	St. Regis-Sheraton	77	French	55+	753-4500
Kurumazushi	18 W 56th	60	Sushi	40-50	541-9030
L'Endroit	208 E 52nd St	112	Fr/Contl	35-40	759-7373
L'Escargot	47 W 55th St	64	French	20-25	245-4266

★ Prices do not include drinks or gratuities

23

MIDTOWN RESTAURANTS Continued

Restaurant	Address	Map No.	Cuisine	Average Price ★	Telephone
L'Incontro	307 E 45th St	171	N. Italian	$35-40	697-9664
L'Omnibus de Maxim	680 Madison Ave	15	Continental	20-25	980-6988
La Bibliotheque	341 E 43rd St	178	Continental	25-35	661-5757
La Camelia	225 E 58th St	37	N. Italian	35-45	751-5488
La Caravelle	33 W 55th St	66	French	51.00	586-4252
La Cote Basque	5 E 55th St	67	French	48.00	688-6525
La Cour St Germain	1059 Third Ave	13	French	30-35	593-4910
La Fondue	43 W 55th St	64	Swiss Fr	12-18	581-0820
La Galerie	Omni Berkshire	99	French	30-37	753-5970
La Grenouille	3 E 52nd St	98	French	65 +	752-1495
La Mangeoire	1008 Second Ave	93	French	30-35	759-7086
La Mediterranee	947 Second Ave	123	French	20-25	755-4155
La Reserve	4 W 49th St	138	French	48.00	247-2993
La Table des Rois	135 E 50th St	118	French	30-35	223-8655
Lafayette	Drake Swissotel	52	French	55 +	832-1565
Laurent	111 E 56th St	56	French	30-45	753-2729
Le Bistro	827 Third Ave	119	French	20-25	759-5933
Le Bistro d'Adrienne	Maxim's Hotel	65	French	35-40	247-2200
Le Chantilly	106 E 57th St	55	French	37.50	751-2931
Le Cheval Blanc	145 E 45th St	165	French	19-25	599-8886
Le Cirque	58 E 65th St	3	French	55-60	794-9292
Le Cygne	55 E 54th St	79	French	56.00	759-5941
Le Festival	134 E 61st St	20	Seafood	40.00	838-7987
Le Manoir	120 E 56th St	68	French	15-25	753-1447
Le Perigord	405 E 52nd St	106	French	45-55	755-6244
Le Regence	Plaza Athenee	4	French	57.50	734-9100
Le Steak	1089 Second Ave	47	French	35-40	421-9072
Le Trianon	Helmsley Palace	115	Continental	50 +	888-7000
Le Veau d'Or	129 E 60th St	22	French	25-30	838-8133
Lello	65 E 54th St	80	Italian	30-45	751-1555
Leopard	253 E 50th St	124	French	43.00	759-3735
Les Sans-Culottes	1085 Second Ave	48	French	15-20	838-6660
Les Tournebroches	Citicorp Center	89	French	10-19	935-6029
Louise Jr.	317 E 53rd St	94	N. Italian	18-26	355-9172
Lutece	249 E 50th St	122	French	58.00	752-2225
Madame Romaine	29 E 61st St	16	French	25-30	758-2422
Manhattan Ocean	57 W 58th	35	Seafood	35-45	371-7777
Maxim's	680 Madison Ave	15	French	45-55	751-5111
Maxwell's Plum	1181 First Ave	7	American	30-35	628-2100
Menage a Trois	Lexington Hotel	150	French	30-40	593-8242
Michael's Pub	211 E 55th St	74	American	15-25	758-2272
Mickey Mantle's	42 Central Pk S	33	American	30-40	688-7777
Mitsukoshi	465 Park Ave	53	Japanese	25-35	935-6444
Miyako	20 W 56th St	59	Japanese	15-20	265-3177
Nada Sushi	135 E 50th St	118	Sushi	25-30	838-2537
Nanni	146 E 46th St	162	Italian	45-50	697-4161
Nibbles	501 Lexington Ave	151	American	18-25	838-7979
Nippon	155 E 52nd St	111	Japanese	25-35	688-5941
Nirvana	30 Central Pk S	33	Indian	20-30	486-5700
Nyborg & Nelson	Citcorp Center	89	Scandvn	10-15	223-0700
Oak Room	Plaza Hotel	34	American	40-45	546-5330
Orsini's	26 E 63rd St	9	French	50 +	752-1750
Oscar's	Citicorp Center	89	Seafood	15-20	371-2201
Oyster Bar	Grand Central	176	Seafood	20-35	490-6650
PJ Clark's	915 Third Ave	71	American	13-18	759-1650
Palm	837 Second Ave	172	Steak	30-35	687-2953

24

★ *Prices do not include drinks or gratuities*

Restaurant	Address	Map No.	Cuisine	Average Price ★	Telephone
Palm Too	840 Second Ave	174	American	$45 +	697-5198
Park Room	Park Lane Hotel	33	Continental	45 +	371-4000
Pearl's Chinese	38 W 48th	147	Chinese	20-35	221-6677
Peccavi	251 E 52nd	103	American	20-25	753-6387
Pen & Pencil	205 E 45th St	168	Steak/Sfd	20-35	682-8660
Petrossian Restaurant	182 W 58th St	off map	French	42-110	245-2214
Pierre Hotel Cafe	Fifth Ave & 61st	19	Fr/Cont	45 +	838-8000
Pietro's	232 E 43rd St	177	Italian/Stk	45 +	682-9760
Polo	Westbury Hotel	off map	Fr Continent	55 +	535-9141
Post House, The	28 E 63rd	10	American	40-50	935-2888
Press Box	139 E 45th St	164	Ital Contl	20-25	697-4734
Primola	1226 Second Ave	5	No. Italian	30-40	758-1775
Pronto	30 E 60th St	26	Italian	20-25	421-8151
Prunelle	18 E 54th St	87	French	56.00	759-6410
Quaglino's	783 Fifth Ave	25	N. Italian	50 +	759-9047
Quilted Giraffe	Madison & 55th	78	Amer Luxury	75-100	593-1221
Rainbow Room	30 Rockefeller Plz	127	Continental	40-60	632-5100
Raphael	33 W 54th St	76	French	35-45	582-8993
Regine	502 Park Ave	27	French	49.50	826-0990
Rendez-Vous	21 E 52nd St	99	Continental	25-30	753-5970
Romeo Salta	30 W 56th St	58	Italian	45 +	246-5772
Sagano	3 E 44th	158	Japanese	30-45	986-1355
San Giusto	935 Second Ave	135	N. Italian	30-40	319-0900
San Marco	36 W 52nd St	107	Italian	25-30	246-5340
Sandro's	420 E 59th	41	Italian	40-50	355-5150
Scarlatti's	34 E 52nd	110	Regional Ital	30-45	753-2444
Sea Grill	Rockfeller Center	126	Seafood	40-50	246-9201
Seryna	11 E 53rd	88	Japanese	40-45	980-9393
Shinbashi	280 Park Ave	143	Japanese	25-35	661-3915
Shun Lee Palace	155 E 55th St	72	Chinese	30-35	371-8844
Sichuan Pavilion	310 E 44th St	179	Chinese	25-30	972-7377
Sign of the Dove	1110 Third Ave	1	Continental	55 +	861-8080
Smith & Wolensky	201 E 49th St	134	Steak	45-50	753-1530
Spark's Steakhouse	210 E 46th St	166	Steak	30-40	687-4855
Stouffer's	666 Fifth Ave	96	Amer Contl	20-30	757-6662
Sushiden	19 E 49th St	128	Japanese	25-30	758-2700
Takesushi	71 Vanderbilt	159	Japan/Sushi	20-25	867-5120
Tandoor	40 E 49th St	141	Indian	25-30	752-3334
Tang's Chariot	236 E 53rd	102	Szechuan	20-30	355-5096
Terrace, The	Trump Tower	51	French	30-35	371-5030
Tino's	235 E 58th St	38	Italian	30-35	751-0311
Tonino	805 Third Ave	134	N. Italian	30-35	308-2280
Top of the Sixes	666 Fifth Ave	95	Amer Cont	25-35	757-6662
Torremolinos	230 E 51st St	121	Spanish	25-30	755-1862
Toscana	200 E 54th St	90	No Italian	30-35	371-8144
Trattoria	Pan Am Bldg	160	Italian	15-20	661-3090
Tre Scalini	230 E 58th St	45	Italian	35-45	688-6888
Trumpet's	Grand Hyatt Hotel	177	American	40-45	850-5999
Tse Yang	34 E 51st	114	Chinese	55 +	688-5447
21 Club	21 W 52nd St	97	Continental	50 +	582-7200
Waldorf-Peacock Alley	301 Park Ave	130	Continental	25-35	872-4895
Water Club	East River/30th	off map	Amer/Sfd	55 +	683-3333
Weston's	131 E 54th St	81	American	25-30	355-3640
Wylie's Ribs & Co	891 First Ave	125	Texas	25-30	751-0700
Yellowfingers	Third Ave & 60th	28	Calif Ital	20-25	751-8615
Zapata	330 E 53rd St	105	Mexican	8-14	223-9408

★ Prices do not include drinks or gratuities

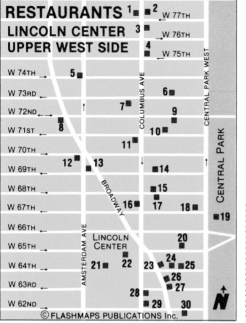

RESTAURANTS
LINCOLN CENTER
UPPER WEST SIDE

1 Museum Cafe
2 Bud's
3 Dobsons
4 Memphis
5 Coastal
6 La Tablita
7 Cavaliere
8 Mrs J's Sacred Cow
9 Sidewalkers
10 Jasmin's Era
11 Victor's Cafe 52
12 Cafe Luxembourg
13 Peking Duck W
14 Santa Fe
15 La Boite
16 Cameos
17 Cafe Destinn
18 Cafe des Artistes
19 Tavern on the Green
20 Shun Lee
21 Grand Tier
22 Allegro Cafe
23 Saloon, The
24 Ginger Man
25 Arpeggio's
26 Fiorello's
27 Houlihan's
28 O'Neal's Baloon
29 Columbus Grill
30 Top of the Park

© FLASHMAPS PUBLICATIONS Inc.

RESTAURANTS—LINCOLN CENTER / UPPER WEST SIDE

Restaurant	Address	Map No	Cuisine	Avg Price ★	Telephone
Allegro Cafe	Lincoln Center	22	American	$25-30	874-7000
Arpeggio's	35 W 64th Street	25	Cont/Seafd	18-25	724-0103
Bud's	359 Columbus Ave	2	California	15-25	724-2100
Cafe Destinn	70 W 68th Street	17	Continental	25-30	496-2144
Cafe Luxembourg	200 W 70th Street	12	Fr/Amer	28-35	873-7411
Cafe des Artistes	1 W 67th Street	18	Prov French	25-35	877-3500
Cameos	169 Columbus Ave	16	New Amer	25-35	874-2280
Cavaliere	108 W 73rd St	7	N. Italian	30-35	799-8282
Coastal	300 Columbus Ave	5	Seafood	25-30	769-3988
Columbus Grill	Columbus & 62nd St	29	American	28-35	586-1222
Dobsons	341 Columbus Ave	3	American	10-20	362-0100
Fiorello's	1900 Broadway	26	Italian	25-30	595-5330
Ginger Man	51 W 64th Street	24	Continental	25-35	399-2358
Grand Tier	Metropolitan Opera	21	Continental	45-50	799-3400
Houlihan's	1900 Broadway	27	American	10-15	362-1340
Jasmin's Era	73 W 71st Street	10	Szechuan	10-15	877-1400
La Boite en Bois	75 W 68th St	15	French	25-30	874-2705
La Tablita	65 W 73rd Street	6	Argen/Ital	20-25	724-9595
Memphis	329 Columbus Ave	4	Regionl Amer	25-35	496-1840
Mrs J's Sacred Cow	228 W 72nd Street	8	American	25-35	873-4067
Museum Cafe	366 Columbus Ave	1	American	10-20	799-0150
O'Neal's Baloon	48 W 63rd Street	28	American	6-12	399-2353
Peking Duck West	Amsterdam & 69th St	13	Peking	15-20	799-5457
Saloon, The	1920 Broadway	23	Varied	10-15	874-1500
Santa Fe	72 W 69th St	14	SW Amer	25-30	724-0822
Shun Lee	43 W 65th Street	20	Chinese	30-35	595-8895
Sidewalkers	12 W 72nd Street	9	Seafood	15-25	799-6070
Tavern-on-the-Green	Central Pk W & 67th	19	Amer/Cont	40-45	873-3200
Top of the Park	1 Gulf Western Plz	30	French/Ital	35-40	373-7373
Victor's Cafe 71	Columbus & 71st St	11	Cuban	15-20	877-7988

★ Prices do not include drinks or gratuities

1 Cafe du Soir
2 Trastevere
3 Le Refuge
4 Ottomanellis
5 Primavera
6 Ristorante Dieci
7 Terrace Dining Rm
8 Gibbon
9 Sistina
10 Diva
11 Pig Heaven
12 Jams
13 Giancarlo
14 Pancho Villa's
15 L'Oustalet
16 Lusardi's
17 Carlyle
18 Csarda
19 Il Monello
20 Brighton Grill
21 Bravo Sergio
22 Vasata
23 Cafe San Martin
24 Mortimer's
25 Vivolo
26 Andree's
27 Petaluma
28 Marcello
29 La Petite Ferme
30 American Place

© FLASHMAPS PUBLICATIONS Inc.

RESTAURANTS—UPPER EAST SIDE

Restaurant	Address	Map No	Cuisine	Avg Price ★	Telephone
American Place	969 Lexington	30	American	$58.00	517-7660
Andree's	354 E 74th	26	Mediterran	30-35	249-6619
Bravo Sergio	1452 Second Ave	21	Italian	20-25	772-3629
Brighton Grill	1313 Third Ave	20	Seafood	30-35	988-6663
Cafe du Soir	322 E 86th	1	French	17-23	427-3900
Cafe San Martin	1458 First Ave	23	Spanish	20-30	288-0470
Carlyle Restaurant	983 Madison Ave	17	Fr/Contl	35-45	744-1600
Csarda	1477 2nd Ave	18	Hungarian	20-25	472-2892
Diva	306 E 81st	10	N. Italian	35-45	650-1928
Elaine's	1703 2nd Ave	off map	Italian	45+	534-8103
Giancarlo	1378 Third Ave	13	Italian	25-30	734-0005
Gibbon	24 E 80th	8	Japan/Fr	40+	861-4001
Il Monello	1460 2nd Ave	19	N. Italian	25-35	535-9310
Jams	154 E 79th St	12	California	30-40	772-6800
L'Oustalet	448 E 79th	15	French	35-45	249-4920
La Petite Ferme	973 Lexington	29	French	40-45	249-3272
Le Refuge	166 E 82nd St	3	French	35-40	861-4505
Lusardi's	1494 Second Ave	16	Italian	25-30	249-2020
Marcello	1354 First Ave	28	N. Italian	25-35	744-4400
Mortimer's	1057 Lexington	24	American	25-35	517-6400
Ottomanellis Stkhouse	439 E 82nd St	4	Game/Stk	25-35	744-9600
Pancho Villa's	1501 2nd Ave	14	Mexican	15-20	650-1455
Petaluma	1356 1st Ave	27	Varied	20-30	772-8800
Pig Heaven	1540 Second Ave	11	Chinese	15-25	744-4333
Primavera	1578 First Ave	5	N. Italian	50+	861-8608
Ristorante Dieci	1568 First Ave	6	Italian	30-45	628-6565
Sistina	1555 Second Ave	9	Italian	40-50	861-7660
Terrace Dining Room	Stanhope Hotel	7	Continental	55.00	288-5800
Trastevere	309 E 83rd St	2	Italian	25-30	734-6343
Vasata	339 E 75th	22	Czech	20-25	650-1686
Vivolo	140 E 74th	25	Italian	15-25	737-3533

★ Prices do not include drinks or gratuities

27

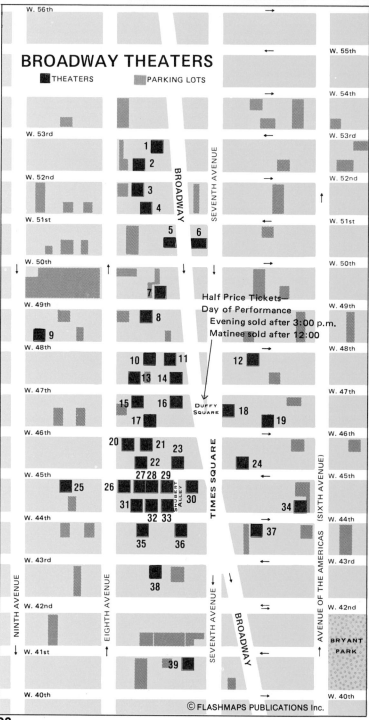

BROADWAY THEATERS

■ THEATERS   ■ PARKING LOTS

Half Price Tickets—
Day of Performance
Evening sold after 3:00 p.m.
Matinee sold after 12:00

DUFFY SQUARE

TIMES SQUARE

SHUBERT ALLEY

BRYANT PARK

BROADWAY

SEVENTH AVENUE

NINTH AVENUE

EIGHTH AVENUE

AVENUE OF THE AMERICAS (SIXTH AVENUE)

W. 56th
W. 55th
W. 54th
W. 53rd
W. 52nd
W. 51st
W. 50th
W. 49th
W. 48th
W. 47th
W. 46th
W. 45th
W. 44th
W. 43rd
W. 42nd
W. 41st
W. 40th

© FLASHMAPS PUBLICATIONS Inc.

28

BROADWAY THEATERS—BY MAP NUMBERS

1 Broadway	10 Longrace	20 Imperial	30 Minskoff
2 Virginia	11 Ritz	21 46th Street	31 Majestic
3 Neil Simon	12 Cort	22 Music Box	32 Broadhurst
4 Mark Hellinger	13 Biltmore	23 Marquis	33 Shubert
5 Circle in Sq	14 Barrymore	24 Lyceum	34 Belasco
5 Gershwin	15 Brooks Atkinson	25 Martin Beck	35 St. James
6 Winter Garden	16 Edison	26 Golden	36 Helen Hayes
7 Ambassador	17 Lunt & Fontanne	27 Royale	37 Lamb's
8 Eugene O'Neill	18 Palace	28 Plymouth	39 Nederlander
9 Jack Lawrence	19 American Place	29 Booth	

BROADWAY THEATERS—ALPHABETICAL

Theater	Address	Seats	Map No.	Telephones ★
Ambassador	215 W 49th	1125	7	TELE-CHARGE
American Place	111 W 46th	300	19	246-3730
Barrymore, Ethel	243 W 47th	1096	14	TELE-CHARGE
Belasco	111 W 44th	923	34	TELE-CHARGE
Biltmore	261 W 47th	949	13	NO PHONE
Booth	222 W 45th	783	29	TELE-CHARGE, TICKETRON
Broadhurst	235 W 44th	1157	32	TELE-CHARGE, TICKETRON
Broadway	1681 Broadway	1765	1	TELE-CHARGE, TICKETRON
Brooks Atkinson	256 W 47th	1090	15	719-4099
Circle in Sq Uptown	1633 Broadway	648	5	TELE-CHARGE 307-2700
Cort	138 W 48th	1089	12	TELE-CHARGE, TICKETRON
Edison	240 W 47th	505	16	TELETRON, TICK 302-2302
Eugene O'Neill	230 W 49th	1062	8	TICKETRON 246-0220
46th Street	226 W 46th	1321	21	TELETRON, TICKETRON
Gershwin	222 W 51st	1933	5	TELETRON/tick 586-6510
Golden	252 W 45th	805	26	TELE-CHARGE
Helen Hayes	240 W 44th	499	36	TELETRON/tick 944-9450
Imperial	249 W 45th	1452	20	TELE-CHARGE, TICKETRON
Jack Lawrence	359 W 48th	499	9	307-5452
Lamb's	130 W 44th	499	37	997-1780
Longacre	220 W 48th	1096	10	TELE-CHARGE
Lunt & Fontanne	205 W 46th	1478	17	TELETRON 575-9200
Lyceum	149 W 45th	928	24	TELE-CHARGE
Majestic	247 W 44th	1629	31	TELE-CHARGE/TICK 246-0730
Mark Hellinger	237 W 51st	1603	4	TICK/TCHRG/TRON 757-7050
Marquis	1700 Broadway	1460	23	TELE-CHARGE, TELE/TICK
Martin Beck	302 W 45th	1260	25	TELETRON 246-6363
Minskoff	B'way & 45th	1621	30	TELETRON/tick 869-0550
Music Box	239 W 45th	1010	22	TELE-CHARGE/tick 246-4636
Nederlander	208 W 41st	1168	39	TICKETRON 921-8000
Neil Simon	250 W 52nd	1334	3	TELETRON/tick 757-8646
Palace	B'way & 47th	1686	18	TELETRON 757-2626
Plymouth	236 W 45th	1077	28	TELE-CHARGE, TICKETRON
Ritz	219 W 48th	499	11	TELETRON/tick 582-4022
Royale	242 W 45th	1059	27	TELE-CHARGE, TICKETRON
St. James	246 W 44th	1559	35	TELETRON/tick 398-0280
Shubert	225 W 44th	1483	33	TELETRON, TICKETRON
Virginia	245 W 52nd	1342	2	977-9370
Winter Garden	1634 Broadway	1518	6	TELE-CHARGE, TICKETRON

LINCOLN CENTER (SEE PAGE 56)

Mitzi Newhouse 362-7600   Vivian Beaumont 787-6868

★ Tele-Charge 239-5850   Teletron 947-0333   Ticketron 399-4444

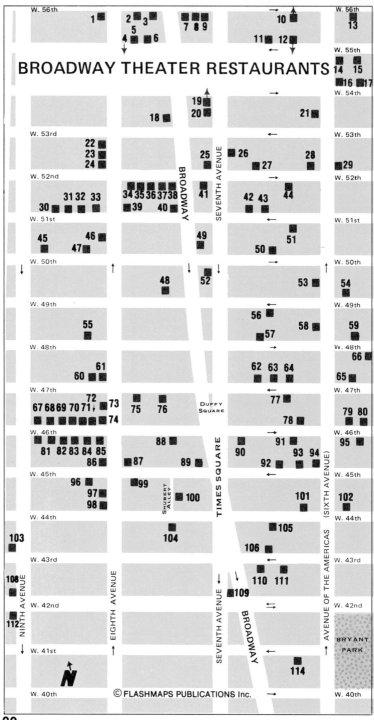

BROADWAY THEATER RESTAURANTS

BROADWAY THEATER RESTAURANTS—BY MAP NOS.

1 Coq au Vin	38 Wine Bistro	77 Fundador
2 D'Angelo's	39 Les Pyrenees	78 Le Vert Galant
3 El Jerez	40 Beefsteak Charlie	79 Woo Lae Oak
4 Caramba	41 King of the Sea	80 Brazilian Coffee
5 Jose Sent Me	42 Le Bernardin	81 Audrone's
6 Sushiko	43 Palio	81 Fontana Rosa
7 India Pavilion	44 Sam's	82 Cafe de France
8 Fuji	45 Chez Napoleon	83 Le Rivage
9 Patsy's	46 La Grillade	84 Joe Allen's
10 Maurice	47 Seeda Thai	85 Orso
11 Cafe Betw Breads	48 Wally's	86 Kodama
12 Castellano	49 Hawaii Kai	87 Frankie & Johnnie
12 Tastings	50 Ho Ho	88 Pergola
13 Darbar	51 Uncle Sam's	89 View, The
14 Le Quercy	52 Bellini	90 Celestial Empire
15 La Bonne Soupe	53 Lindy's	91 La Strada
16 Sir Walter's	54 Hurley's	92 Johnnie's Italian
17 Raphael	55 Rosa's Place	93 Cabana Carioca II
18 China Song	56 Iroha	94 Cabana Carioca
19 Carnegie Deli	57 Frere Jacques	95 Kitcho New York
19 Larre II	58 Beanstalk	96 Encore Encore
20 Stage Delicatessen	59 Raga	97 Beefsteak Charlie
21 Hurlingham's	60 Trixies	98 Barking Fish
22 Bangkok Cuisine	61 B Smith's	99 Mamma Leone's
23 Caffe Cielo	62 Spirits	100 Charlie O's
24 King Crab	63 La Veranda	101 Cafe Un Deux Trois
25 Rosie O'Grady	64 Dish of Salt	102 Algonquin
26 Rainier's	65 Hong Kong Inn	103 Le Madeleine
27 Pier 52	66 Pearl's Chinese	104 Sardi's
28 Ben Benson's	67 Crepes Suzette	105 China Bowl
29 China Grill	68 Lattanzi	106 Cafe 43
30 Cafe des Sports	69 Carolina	108 West Bank Cafe
31 Rene Pujol	70 La Vieille Auberge	109 Nirvana
32 Cheshire Cheese	71 Barbetta	110 India Dining
33 Tout Va Bien	72 Broadway Joe	111 Century Cafe
34 Russian Samovar	73 Jimmy Ray's	112 Chez Josephine
35 Victor's Cafe	74 La Rivista Palatine	112 Cirella's
36 Gallagher's	75 Delsomma	114 Cheers
37 Broadway Brasserie	76 Pierre au Tunnel	

BROADWAY THEATER RESTAURANTS—ALPHABETICAL

Restaurant	Address	Map No.	Cuisine	Avg Dinner Price ★	Telephone
Algonquin	59 W 44th	102	American	$30-40	840-6800
Audrone's	342 W 46th	81	Fr/Contl	15-25	246-1960
B Smith's	771 Eighth Ave	61	American	20-25	247-2222
Bangkok Cuisine	885 Eighth Ave	22	Thai	15-20	581-6370
Barbetta	321 W 46th	71	N. Italian	35-45	246-9171
Barking Fish Cafe	705 Eighth Ave	98	Seafood	20-25	757-0186
Beanstalk	1221 Ave of Amer	58	Vegetarian	15-20	997-1005
Beefsteak Charlie	709 Eighth Ave	97	Steak	10-15	581-0500
Beefsteak Charlie	Broadway at 51st	40	Steak	10-15	757-3110
Bellini	777 Seventh Ave	52	N. Italian	42-50	265-7770
Ben Benson's	123 W 52nd St	28	American	40 +	581-8888
Brazilian Coffee	45 W 46th	80	Brazil/Portg	15-20	719-2105
Broadway Brasserie	226 W 52nd	37	French	15-20	315-0100

★ Prices do not include drinks or gratuities

Restaurant	Address	Map No.	Cuisine	Avg Dinner Price ★	Telephone
Broadway Joe	315 W 46th	72	American	$25-30	246-6513
Cabana Carioca	123 W 45th	94	Brazil/Portg	15-20	581-8088
Cabana Carioca II	133 W 45th	93	Brazil/Portg	15-20	730-8375
Cafe Between Breads	145 W 55th	11	American	20-25	581-1189
Cafe Un Deux Trois	123 W 44th	101	Fr/Amer	25-30	354-4148
Cafe de France	330 W 46th	82	French	17.50	586-0088
Cafe des Sports	329 W 51st	30	French	20-30	974-9052
Cafe 43	147 W 43rd	106	French	13-15	869-4200
Caffe Cielo	881 Eighth Ave	23	N. Italian	30-40	246-9555
Caramba!	918 Eighth Ave	4	Tex-Mex	20-25	245-7910
Carnegie Deli	854 Seventh Ave	19	Deli	12-15	757-2245
Carolina	355 W 46th	69	Regionl Amer	35-40	245-0058
Castellano	138 W 55th	12	Italian	40+	664-1975
Celestial Empire	144 W 46th	90	Cantonese	10-15	869-9183
Century Cafe	132 W 43rd	111	American	20-25	398-1988
Charley O's	45 Shubert Alley	100	Irish/Amer	18-23	840-2964
Cheers	120 W 41st	114	Ital/Amer	20-25	840-8810
Cheshire Cheese	319 W 51st	32	English	27-45	765-0616
Chez Josephine	414 W 42nd	112	Internatl	30-35	594-1925
Chez Napoleon	365 W 50th	45	French	20-25	265-6980
China Bowl	152 W 44th	105	Chinese	10-15	582-3358
China Grill	51 W 52 (CBS bldg)	29	Fr/Calif	35-40	333-7788
China Song	1705 Broadway	18	Cantonese	12-20	246-6759
Cirella's	400 W 42nd St	112	Ital/Contl	20-30	564-0004
Coq au Vin	304 W 56th St	1	French	20-25	541-8273
Crepes Suzette	363 W 46th	67	French	17-25	581-9717
D'Angelo's	242 W 56th	2	Italian	25-30	247-1070
Darbar	44 W 56th	13	Indian	30-35	432-7227
Delsomma	266 W 47th	75	Italian	19.50	719-4179
Devereux's	160 Central Pk S	off map	American	35+	247-0300
Dish of Salt	133 W 47th	64	Cantonese	25-30	921-4242
El Jerez	234 W 56th	3	Span/Mex	12-20	765-4535
Encore Encore	318 W 45th	96	Amer/Fr	27.00	489-6100
Fontana Rosa	344 W 46th	81	Italian	15-20	765-2251
Frankie & Johnnie	269 W 45th	87	American	30-35	997-9494
Frere Jacques	151 W 48th	57	French	15-25	575-1866
Fuji	238 W 56th	8	Japanese	15-25	245-8594
Fundador	146 W 47th	77	Spanish	15-25	819-0012
Gallagher's	228 W 52nd	36	Steak	35-40	245-5336
Hard Rock Cafe	221 W 57th St	off map	American	15-20	489-6565
Hawaii Kai	Broadway & 50th	49	Polynesian	12-20	757-0900
Ho Ho	131 W 50th	50	Chinese	12-20	246-3256
Hong Kong Inn	33 W 47th	65	Chinese	10-20	382-0230
Hurley's	1240 Ave of Amer	54	American	20-25	765-8981
Hurlingham's	Hilton Hotel	21	Steak/Sfd	20-35	265-1600
India Dining	102 W 43rd	110	Indian	8-15	221-6574
Indian Pavilion	240 W 56th	7	Indian	8-12	489-0035
Iroha	142 W 49th St	56	Japanese	10-20	398-9049
Jimmy Ray's	729 Eighth Ave	73	American	12-20	246-8562
Joe Allen's	326 W 46th	84	American	15-25	581-6464
Johnnie's Italian	135 W 45th	92	Italian	15-25	997-9315
Jose Sent Me	253 W 55th	5	Tex Mex	17-23	246-3253
King Crab	871 Eighth Ave	24	Seafood	15-25	765-4393
King of Sea	808 Seventh Ave	41	Seafood	28-35	757-3522
Kitcho New York	22 W 46th	95	Japanese	20-25	575-8880
Kodama	301 W 45th	86	Japanese	13-17	582-8065

★ *Prices do not include drinks or gratuities*

BROADWAY THEATER RESTAURANTS Continued

Restaurant	Address	Map No.	Cuisine	Avg Dinner Price ★	Telephone
La Bonne Soupe	48 W 55th	15	French	$10-15	586-7650
La Grillade	845 Eighth Ave	46	French	20-30	265-1610
La Rivista Palatine	313 W 46th St	74	Italian	35-40	245-1707
La Strada	134 W 46th	91	Italian	22-25	382-0060
La Veranda	163 W 47th St	63	Italian	23-25	391-0905
La Vieille Auberge	347 W 46th	70	French	20-25	247-4284
Larre II	846 Seventh	19	French	15-20	586-8096
Lattanzi	361 W 46th	68	Italian	40-50	315-0980
Le Bernardin	155 W 51st St	42	Seafood	60.00	489-1515
Le Madeleine	403 W 43rd	103	French	25-30	246-2993
Le Quercy	52 W 55th	14	French	15-25	265-8141
Le Rivage	340 W 46th	83	French	18-25	765-7374
Le Vert Galant	109 W 46th	78	French	23-28	382-0022
Les Pyrenees	251 W 51st	39	French	20-25	246-0044
Lindy's	1256 Ave of Amer	53	Deli/Steak	10-15	586-8986
Mamma Leone's	Milford Plaza Hotel	99	Italian	20-30	869-3600
Maurice	Htl Parker Meridien	10	French	60-65	245-7788
Nirvana I	One Times Square	109	Indian	20-25	486-6868
Orso	322 W 46th	85	Italian	20-25	489-7212
Palio	151 W 51st	43	Reginl Ital	40-55	245-4850
Patsy's	236 W 56th	9	Italian	25-30	247-3491
Pearl's Chinese	38 W 48th	66	Chinese	25-30	221-6677
Pergola	252 W 46th	88	French	15-20	840-8935
Pier 52	163 W 52nd	27	Seafood	25-35	245-6652
Pierre au Tunnel	250 W 47th St	76	French	20-25	575-1220
Raga	57 W 48th	59	Indian	25-30	757-3450
Rainier's	Sheraton Centre	26	American	30.00	581-1000
Raphael	33 W 54th	17	Lt French	30-40	582-8993
Rene Pujol	321 W 51st	31	French	26-30	246-3023
Rosa's Place	303 W 48th	55	Tex/Mex	12-20	586-4853
Rosie O'Grady	800 Seventh	25	Irish/Contl	20-25	582-2975
Russian Samovar	256 W 52nd	34	Russian	25-30	757-0168
Russian Tea Room	150 W 57th	off map	Russian	30-45	265-0947
Sam's	152 W 52nd St	44	Nouvelle	20-30	582-8700
San Domenico	240 Central Pk S	off map	Italian	50 +	265-5959
Sardi's	234 W 44th	104	Continental	25-35	221-8440
Seeda Thai	309 W 50th St	47	Thai	15-25	586-4040
Sir Walter's	Warwick Hotel	16	Continental	23-25	247-3793
Spirits	165 W 47th	62	Italian	15-20	302-6186
Stage Delicatessen	834 Seventh Ave	20	Jewish	10-15	245-7850
Sushiko	251 W 55th	6	Japanese	10-15	974-9721
Tastings	144 W 55th	12	Varied	20-30	757-1160
Terrace - Butler Hall	Columbia Univ	off map	Fr Classic	60-65	666-9490
Tout Va Bien	311 W 51st	33	French	20-25	265-0190
Trixies	307 W 47th	60	American	10-12	840-9537
Uncle Sam's	120 W 51st	51	American	15-20	757-8800
Victor's Cafe 52	236 W 52nd	35	Cuban	20-25	586-7714
View, The	Marriott Marquis	89	Continental	50-55	704-8900
Wally's	249 W 49th	48	Steak/Sfd	40-45	582-0460
West Bank Cafe	407 W 42nd	108	Continental	15-20	695-6909
Windows on the Wrld	World Trade Ctr	off map	Continental	30-45	938-1111
Wine Bistro	Novotel Hotel	38	American	10-15	315-0100
Woo Lae Oak	77 W 46th	79	Korean	20-30	869-9958

★ Prices do not include drinks or gratuities

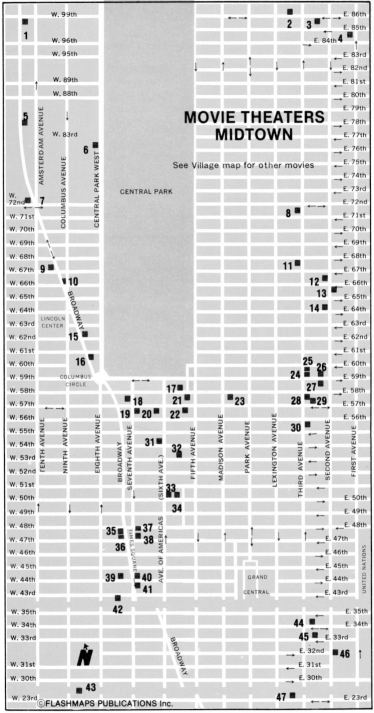

MOVIE THEATERS
MIDTOWN

See Village map for other movies

MOVIES THEATERS—MIDTOWN

ALPHABETICAL

Theater	Map No	Telephone
Baronet	24	355-1664
Bay Cinema	46	679-0160
Beekman	13	737-2622
Biograph	18	582-4582
Carnegie Hall Cinema	19	265-2520
Carnegie Screening Rm	19	757-2131
Cine 1 & 2	36	398-1720
Cinema I	25	753-6022
Cinema II	25	753-0774
Cinema III	17	752-5959
Cinema Studio 1, 2	10	877-4040
Coronet	24	355-1663
Criterion Center 1-6	40	354-0900
D.W. Griffith	26	759-4630
Eastside Cinema	30	755-3020
86th St East	3	249-1144
Embassy 1 46th	37	757-2408
Embassy 72, 1, 2	7	724-6745
Embassy 2, 3, 4	38	730-7262
Festival	22	307-7856
57th St Playhouse	20	581-7360
Gemini I	14	832-1670
Gemini II	14	832-2720
Gotham	28	759-2262
Gramercy	47	475-1660
Guild	34	757-2406
Lincoln Plz Cinema 1,2,3	15	757-2280
Loews Astor Plaza	39	869-8340
Loews 34th Showplace 3	45	532-5544
Loews 84th St 1-6	5	877-3600
Loews NY Twin	12	744-7339
Loews Orpheum 1 & 2	2	289-4607
Loews Paramount	16	247-5070
Loews Tower East	8	879-1313
Manhattan I & II	27	935-6420
Metro Cinema	1	222-1200
Movieland	35	757-8320
Museum Modern Art	32	708-9490
National Twin	41	869-0950
Naturemax-Mus Natural	6	769-5200
Paris	21	688-2013
Plaza	23	355-3320
Radio City Music Hall	33	757-3100
Regency	9	724-3700
68th St Playhouse	11	734-0302
Sutton	29	759-1411
34th St East	44	683-0255
23rd St W Triplex	43	989-0060
United Artist 85th East	4	249-5100
Warner Odeon	42	764-6760
Ziegfeld	31	765-7600

—BY MAP NUMBERS

Map No	Theater
1	Metro
2	Loews Orpheum
3	86th St East
4	U A 85th East
5	Loews 84th 1-6
6	Naturemax
7	Embassy 72 1,2
8	Loews Tower East
9	Regency
10	Cinema Studio 1,2
11	68th St Playhouse
12	Loews NY Twin
13	Beekman
14	Gemini I
14	Gemini II
15	Lincoln Plaza
16	Loews Paramount
17	Cinema III
18	Biograph
19	Carnegie Hall
19	Carnegie Screening
20	57th St
21	Paris
22	Festival
23	Plaza
24	Baronet
24	Coronet
25	Cinema I
25	Cinema II
26	D.W. Griffith
27	Manhattan I,II
28	Gotham
29	Sutton
30	Eastside
31	Ziegfeld
32	Mus Modern Art
33	Radio City
34	Guild
35	Movieland
36	Cine 1 & 2
37	Embassy 1
38	Embassy 2,3,4
39	Loews Astor Plaza
40	Criterion
41	National
42	Warner
43	23rd St
44	34th St East
45	Loews 34th St
46	Bay Cinema
47	Gramercy

OFF MAP:

Film Forum-57 Wall Street	431-1590		Little (Public)-425 Lafayette St	598-7171	
Columbia Cinema-B'way/103rd	316-6660		Coliseum Twin-B'way & 181st	927-7200	
Harlem Movie Ctr-235 W 125th	222-8900		Olympia 1,2-B'way & 107th St	865-8128	

GREENWICH VILLAGE MOVIES PAGE 42

Streets	Central PkW	Broadway	Avenue of the Americas (Sixth Av)	Fifth Av	Madison
95–96	352–360	2540–2556		1140–1148	1356–1379
94–95	341–351	2520–2537		1130–1136	1340–135(
93–94	331–336	2501–2519		1120–1125	1316–1335
92–93	322–327	2478–2500		1109–1115	1295–131?
91–92	315–320	2460–2475		1100–1107	1273–129?
90–91	300	2440–2459		NY Sch. Social Wk.	1254–127?
89–90	293–295	2420–2439	The	1080–1089	1239–125(
88–89	281–285	2400–2418		Guggenheim	1222–123?
87–88	271–275	2380–2398	numbers	1060–1069	1190–122?
86–87	262	2361–2379		1051–1056	1175–119?
85–86	251	2341–2355	of	1040–1048	1150–117?
84–85	241–249	2320–2342		1030–1035	1125–1148
83–84	230–239	2300–2318	nearest	1020–1028	1109–1128
82–83	225–227	2280–2299		1010–1018	1089–109?
81–82	217–219	2260–2279	streets	998–1009	1072–1088
80–81	Planetarium Museum of Natural Hist.	2240–2259		990–997	1050–107?
79–80		2220–2239	will be	980–989	1033–104?
78–79		2200–2219		972–973	1011–102?
77–78		2180–2199	found on	960–969	998–100?
76–77	170	2160–2177		950–956	974–991
75–76	151	2140–2159	the	942–947	954–970
74–75	145	2120–2139		930–936	933–953
73–74	135	2100–2114	lamp-	922–929	917–932
72–73	119	2081–2099		910–920	896–909
71–72	115	2061–2079	posts	900–907	861–872
70–71	101	2040–2062		Frick	845–870
69–70	91–99	2020–2030	in	880–885	828–850
68–69	80–88	2000–2016		870–875	813–827
67–68	75	1990–1999	Central	857–860	793–811
66–67	65–70	1960–1978		854–856	772–790
65–66	55–58	1940–1959	Park	Temple Emanu El	754–771
64–65	41–50	1920–1936		833–838	733–750
63–64	33	Lincoln C.		820–828	710–727
62–63	25	1881–1896	Avenue	810–817	690–709
61–62	13–20	1860–1880	of the	800–807	673–680
60–61	Central Pk	Coliseum	Americas	Central Pk.	654–667
59–60	Columbus C.	Columbus Cir.	(Sixth Av)	790 Hotel Pierre / Grand Army Plz	635–649
	Seventh Av				
58–59	919–933	1796–1806	1420–1439	Gen. Motors	621 Gen. Mo
57–58	901–917	1775–1785	1400–1419	742–754	598–611
56–57	Carnegie Hall	1751–1770	Chase Man. Bk	720–730	572–590
55–56	858–880	1730–1750	1361–1377	707–718	550–568
54–55	841–855	1709–1728	1340–1357	689–703	532–548
53–54	825–838	1691–1707	1330 N.Y. Hilton	673–685	512–531
52–53	800–820 Americana	1671–1687	1301	655–671	500–509
51–52	781–799	1651–1665	1281–1297	640–653	477–488
50–51	761–780	1631–1650	1260–1277 Radio City	St. Patrick's	452–460
49–50	742–760	1612–1630	1240–1258	610–620 Saks Fifth	433–444

Rockefeller Plz

AVENUES FROM 14 TO 96 STREET

Park Av	Lexington Av	Third Av	Second Av	First Av	Streets
1220–1236	1476–1486	1695–1709	1840–1868	1841–1855	**95–96**
1199–1217	1449–1470	1678–1693	1817–1838	1817–1835	**94–95**
1180–1192	1424–1444	1662–1677	1800–1808	1797–1811	**93–94**
1160–1178	1400–1423	1644–1660	1766–1780	1780–1795	**92–93**
1140–1155	1380–1396	1622–1643	1748–1763	1756–1779	**91–92**
1120–1135	1361–1379	1601–1620	1736–1746	1740–1754	**90–91**
1100–1114	1342–1355	1585–1602	1716–1739	1718–1735	**89–90**
1080–1095	1311–1338	1568–1583	1700–1715	1701–1717	**88–89**
1060–1076	1300–1301	1550–1566	1682–1698	1668–1689	**87–88**
1040–1055	1280–1288	1529–1546	1669–1679	1653–1667	**86–87**
1020–1035	1263–1278	1511–1525	1640–1657	1637–1651	**85–86**
1000–1015	1241–1261	1480–1508	1619–1638	1618–1631	**84–85**
980–993	1228–1246	1470–1478	1601–1617	1602–1616	**83–84**
962–970	1211–1226	1453–1469	1583–1598	1577–1593	**82–83**
940–960	1190–1209	1430–1451	1561–1576	1569–1576	**81–82**
920–935	1177–1187	1410–1433	1588–1560	1533–1556	**80–81**
900–911	1141–1161	1390–1406	1522–1536	1514–1528	**79–80**
885–899	1120–1140	1367–1389	1501–1519	1495–1512	**78–79**
860–879	1101–1116	1356–1372	1480–1496	1479–1494	**77–78**
840–850	1079–1090	1329–1347	1456–1477	1462–1475	**76–77**
820–830	1057–1071	1311–1328	1448–1454	1444–1460	**75–76**
799–815	1033–1055	1291–1309	1420–1439	1429–1442	**74–75**
778–791	1019–1032	1271–1285	1403–1417	1370–1384	**73–74**
760–775	1003–1022	1251–1260	1389–1391	1352–1359	**72–73**
737–755	985–993	1230–1248	1339–1363	1325–1340	**71–72**
720–733	962–983		1341–1347	1306–1321	**70–71**
701–715	944–961	1187–1208	1313–1320	1286–1300	**69–70**
680–695	930	1175–1185	1296–1310	1265–1284	**68–69**
660–664	901–922	1150–1165	1283–1297	1246–1260	**67–68**
640–650 Armory	Armory		1260–1281	1224–1239	**66–67**
620–635	868–886	1110–1128	1242–1258	1205–1220	**65–66**
600–610	841–869	1090–1109	1226–1238	1168–1200	**64–65**
580–598	824–842	1066–1089	1210–1220	1152–1166	**63–64**
560–575	803–817	1059–1069	1177–1196	1130–1149	**62–63**
535–555	784–802	1030–1048	1161–1178	1113–1131	**61–62**
520–530	770–782	1011–1029	1140–1159	1097–1112	**60–61**
501–519	738–759	989–1000	Queensboro Br.	Queensboro Br.	**59–60**
480–500	722–741	972–989	1104–1116	1065–1082	**58–59**
460–475	700–721	953–968	1083–1101	1058–1063	**57–58**
434–446	677–698	942–948	1066–1082	1026–1044	**56–57**
425–430	657–665	914–933	1044–1062	1006–1021	**55–56**
400–417	641–652	894–908	1024–1042	984–1003	**54–55**
378–399	617–629	876–895	1003–1027	965–982	**53–54**
370–375	609–615	855–875	984–1002	945–964	**52–53**
341–350	575–593	845–850	964–982	930–944	**51–52**
320–321	557–573	824–835	943–961	891–905	**50–51**
300 Waldorf	538–556	797–816	923–941	883–890	**49–50**

Streets	Seventh Av	Broadway	Sixth Av	Fifth Av	Madison
48–49	721–740	1591–1611	1221–1237	595–609	412–431
47–48	701–720	1571–1590	1201–1217	579–594	400
46–47		1551–1570	1180–1197	562–578	377–385
45–46	Use	1531–1550	1160–1178	546–560	359–375
44–45	Broadway	1511–1530	1140–1156	530–545	341–356
43–44	Numbers	1499–1512	1120–1136	516–529	333–339
42–43		Times Sq	1100–1119	500–514	315–331
41–42	582–598	1451–1470	1081–1097	461–501	299–315
40–41	560–577	1440–1450	1061–1079	Public Lib.	279–298
39–40	545–558	1412–1430	1040–1056	442–462	265–280
38–39	524–530	1400–1410	1020–1036	425–439	260–261
37–38	500–515	1372–1391	1000–1017	411–420	232–245
36–37	486–499	1350–1370	980–996	392–409	218–229
35–36	462–480	1331–1350	960–977	372–390	200–215
34–35	Macy's	Macy's	Herald Sq	355–371 Altman	185–198
33–34	420–440	1282		339–353 Empire State	169–184
32–33	Penn Sta.	1260–1280	Gimbel's	320–334	152–168
	Mad. Sq. G.				
31–32	383–399	1255–1273	875–892	302–316	134–150
30–31	361–377	1220–1251	855–874	282–300	118–133
29–30	341–360	1200–1227	836–844	267–281	99–117
28–29	319–336	1178–1203	815–832	250–264	79–95
27–28	300–320	1158–1181	795–812	233–249	62–78
26–27	282–299	1140–1158	775–793	213–230	50–60
25–26	262–281	1122–1134	755–773	202–212	27–37
24–25	244–261	1101–1117	740–754	Mad. Sq	11–25
23–24	224–240	1097–1099	716–732	200	1–7
22–23	209–220	945–954	695–712	172–186	
21–22	189–208	922–939	675–692	149–170	
20–21	170–185	902–920	655–672	135–160	
19–20	153–169	889–901	635–650	119–150	
18–19	134–145	873–887	615–632	109–140	
17–18	124–133	857–872	592–612	97–128	
16–17	100–116	21–35	574–590	85–116	
15–16	78–98	13–19	552–571	79–108	
14–15	61–77	1–11	530–549	69–96	

(Union Sq W marked between Broadway entries 857–872, 21–35, 13–19, 1–11)

EVEN NUMBER addresses are on the EAST: Broadway, York, West End, Columbus, First, Second, Sixth, Eight, Ninth & Tenth Avenues

ADDRESS FINDER

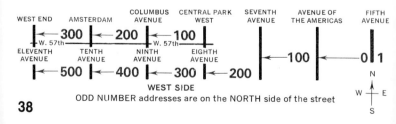

WEST END — 300 → AMSTERDAM — 200 → COLUMBUS AVENUE — 100 → CENTRAL PARK WEST
W. 57th — W. 57th
ELEVENTH AVENUE — 500 → TENTH AVENUE — 400 → NINTH AVENUE — 300 → EIGHTH AVENUE — 200 →

SEVENTH AVENUE   AVENUE OF THE AMERICAS — 100 → FIFTH AVENUE   0 | 1

WEST SIDE
ODD NUMBER addresses are on the NORTH side of the street

N
W ← → E
S

AVENUES FROM 14 TO 96 STS. (Cont'd)

Park Av	Lexington Av	Third Av	Second Av	First Av	Streets
280–299	518–537	776–796	902–922	861–875	**48–49**
270–277	497–515	760–774	883–891	851–U.N.	**47–48**
240–250	480–495	741–755	862–877	827–U.N.	**46–47**
Pan-Am	459–475	721–735	843–860	805–U.N.	**45–46**
Bldg.	441–452	702–716	824–844	785–U.N.	**44–45**
Grand	415–435	684–701	806–823	763–U.N.	**43–44**
Central	400–416	666–679	793–801	park–U.N.	**42–43**
Sta.	374–390	639–655	767–773	Tudor City	**41–42**
100–103	355–373	622–633	747–765	702–720	**40–41**
90–99	334–353	605–618	728–745	686–700	**39–40**
67–80	314–332	579–597	707–724	666–683	**38–39**
49–66	296–311	560–576	685–700	646–662	**37–38**
40–45	281–288	542–558	666–673	Queens Tun.	**36–37**
20–35	264–271	525–541	643–659	624–626	**35–36**
5–17	239–253	507–523	623–641	599–611	**34–35**
3-4 Armory	220–237	488–504	603–621	577–593	**33–34**
1–2	200–218	470–487	585–601		**32–33**
Park Av S				Kips Bay	
461–470	179–196	450–467	563–581	&	**31–32**
444–460	160–178	431–449	543–561	N.Y.U.	**30–31**
424–431	139–159	415–430	524–541	Hospital	**29–30**
403–422	119–138	394–412	500–519	479–Belle-	**28–29**
386–401	99–118	375–391	484–498	463–vue	**27–28**
363–381	81–98	358–365	462–479	445–Hosp.	**26–27**
343–361	61–77	340–355	442–459	429–443	**25–26**
323–341	40–57	321–338	420–437	411–427 Vets.	**24–25**
303–322	21–39	301–318	401–416	393–409 Hosp.	**23–24**
286–308	11–15	288–300	381–398	377–391 Peter	**22–23**
268–285	1–8	266–281	362–380	361–375 Cooper	**21–22**
251–266		244–261	345–361	345–359 Vill.	**20–21**
234–250		226–243	329–343	320–343 Stuy-	**19–20**
221–233		205–222	310–327	313–327 vesant	**18–19**
213–220		187–203	302–308	303–311 Town	**17–18**
184–201		167–177	Stuyvesant	Beth Israel H.	**16–17**
20–34		157–165	Square	259–279	**15–16**
2–18		125–133	321–240	239–257	**14–15**

Left margin labels: Vanderbilt Av, Union Sq E

CROSSTOWN STREETS

MADISON AVENUE	PARK AVENUE	LEXINGTON AVENUE	THIRD AVENUE	SECOND AVENUE	FIRST AVENUE
Half blocks →	100 →	140 →	200 →	300 →	400 →

EAST SIDE

EVEN NUMBER addresses are on the WEST: Amsterdam, Fifth, Third, Seventh, Madison, Park, Lexington Avenues

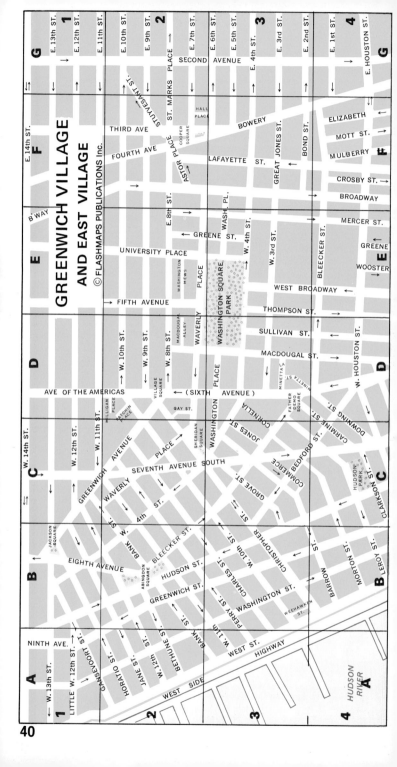

GREENWICH VILLAGE
AND EAST VILLAGE

© FLASHMAPS PUBLICATIONS Inc.

GREENWICH VILLAGE AND EAST VILLAGE STREETS—ALPHABETICAL

Street	Map Location
Abingdon Sq	B-2
Astor Place	F-2
Ave of Americas	D-2
Bank St	A-2
Barrow St	B-4
Bedford St	C-3
Bethune St	A-2
Bleecker St	B-2, E-4
Bond St	F-3
Bowery	F-3
Broadway	E-1, F-4
Carmine St	C-4
Charles St	B-3
Christopher St	B-3
Clarkson St	C-4
Commerce St	C-3
Cooper Sq	F-2
Cornelia St	D-3
Crosby St	F-4
Downing St	C-4
Eighth Ave	B-2
Eighth St E	E-2
Eighth St W	D-2
Eleventh St E	G-1
Eleventh St W	C-1, A-3
Elizabeth St	F-4
Father Demo Sq	D-3
Fifth Ave	E-2
Fifth St E	G-3
First St E	G-4
Fourth Ave	F-2
Fourth St E	G-3
Fourth St W	E-3, C-2
Fourteenth St E	F-1
Fourteenth St W	C-1
Gansevoort St	A-1
Gay St	D-2
Great Jones St	F-3
Greene St	E-2, E-4
Greenwich Ave	C-1
Greenwich St	B-4
Grove St	C-3
Hall Pl	F-2
Horatio St	A-2
Houston St E	G-4
Houston St W	D-4
Hudson Park	C-4
Hudson St	B-2
Jackson Sq	B-1
Jane St	A-2
Jones St	C-3
Lafayette St	F-3
Leroy St	B-4
Little W 12 St	A-1
Macdougal Alley	D-2
Macdougal St	D-3
Mercer St	E-4
Milligan Pl	D-2
Minetta La	D-3
Minetta St	D-3
Morton St	B-4
Mott St	F-4
Mulberry St	F-4
Ninth Ave	A-1
Ninth St E	G-2
Ninth St W	D-2
Patchin Pl	D-2
Perry St	B-3
St Mark's Pl	F-2
Second Ave	G-2
Second St E	G-3
Seventh Ave S	C-2
Seventh St E	G-2
Sheridan Sq	C-2
Sixth Ave	D-2
Sixth St E	G-3
Stuyvesant St	F-2
Sullivan St	D-3
Tenth St E	G-2
Tenth St W	D-2, B-3
Third Ave	F-2
Third St E	G-3
Third St W	E-3
Thirteenth St E	G-1
Thirteenth St W	A-1
Thompson St	E-3
Twelfth St E	G-1
Twelfth St W	C-1, A-2
University Pl	E-2
Village Sq	D-2
Washington Mews	E-2
Washington Pl	C-3
Washington Sq	D, E-3
Washington St	B-3
Waverly Pl	D, E-2, C-2
Weehawken St	B-3
West Broadway	E-3, 4
West SideHwy	A-2, 3
West St	A-3
Wooster St	E-4

Crosstown numbers increase from Fifth Ave toward both rivers. Avenue numbers begin at 0 at Houston St and go up to 250 at 14 St.

41

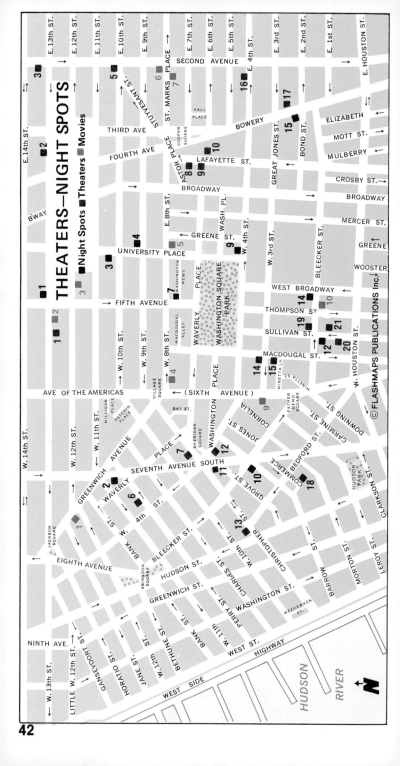

THEATERS—NIGHT SPOTS

■ Night Spots ■ Theaters ■ Movies

© FLASHMAPS PUBLICATIONS Inc.

GREENWICH VILLAGE MOVIES

Theater	Address	Map No	Telephone
Art Greenwich Twin	Greenwich & 12th Street	1	929-3350
Bleecker Street 1 & 2	144 Bleecker Street	10	674-2560
Cinema Village	22 East 12th Street	3	924-3363
8th St Playhouse	52 West 8th Street	4	674-6515
Essex	Grand Street at Essex	off map	982-4455
Little Theater	425 Lafayette Street	6	598-7150
Movieland 1, 2, 3	University Place & E 8th St	5	477-6600
Quad Cinema 1,2,3,4	34 West 13th Street	2	255-8800
Thalia SoHo	15 Van Dam betw 6th & 7th	off map	675-0498
Theater 80 St Marks	80 St Marks Place	7	254-7400
Waverly 1 & 2	Sixth Avenue & 3rd Street	9	929-8037

GREENWICH VILLAGE NIGHT SPOTS

Night Spot	Address	Map No	Telephone
Bitter End	149 Bleecker Street	14	673-7030
Bottom Line Cabaret	15 West 4th Street	9	228-6300
Bradley's	70 University Place	3	228-6440
CBGB	315 Bowery	15	473-7743
Knickerbocker Saloon	33 University Place	4	228-8490
Lone Star Cafe	61 Fifth Avenue	1	242-1664
One Fifth Avenue	Fifth Avenue & 8th Street	7	260-3434
Palladium	126 East 14th Street	off map	473-7171
Ritz	119 East 12th Street	under label	254-2800
Sweet Basil	88 Seventh Avenue South	10	242-1785
Village Corner	142 Bleecker Street	12	473-9762
Village Gate	Bleecker & Thompson St	13	475-5120
Village Vanguard	178 Seventh Ave S at 11th	2	255-4037

OFF BROADWAY THEATERS

Theater	Address	Map No	Telephone
Actors Playhouse	100 Seventh Ave South	11	691-6226
Astor Place Playhouse	434 Lafayette	8	254-4370
Cherry Lane	38 Commerce	18	989-2020
Circle in Square D'town	159 Bleecker	19	254-6330
Circle Repertory Co.	99 Seventh Ave South	12	924-7100
CSC Repertory	136 E 13th Street	2	677-4210
Fourth Wall Rep	79 E 4th Street	16	254-5060
Jazz Center	380 Lafayette	9	505-5660
Jean Cocteau Repertory	330 Bowery	17	677-0060
La Mama	74 E 4th Street	16	475-7710
Lucille Lortel	121 Christopher	13	924-8782
Minetta Lane	18 Minetta Lane	15	420-8000
Orpheum	126 Second Ave	5	477-2477
Players	115 Macdougal	15	254-5076
Perry Street	31 Perry Street	6	255-7190
Provincetown Playhouse	133 Macdougal	14	477-5048
Public Theater Complex (5 thea)	425 Lafayette	10	598-7150
Ridiculous Theater	1 Sheridan Square	7	691-2271
Second Ave	189 Second Ave	3	674-1460
Sullivan Street	181 Sullivan	20	674-3838
13th Street	50 W 13th Street	1	675-6677
Top of the Gate	160 Bleecker Street	21	475-5120

OFF BROADWAY THEATERS (not on map page 46)
BROADWAY THEATERS PAGE 28

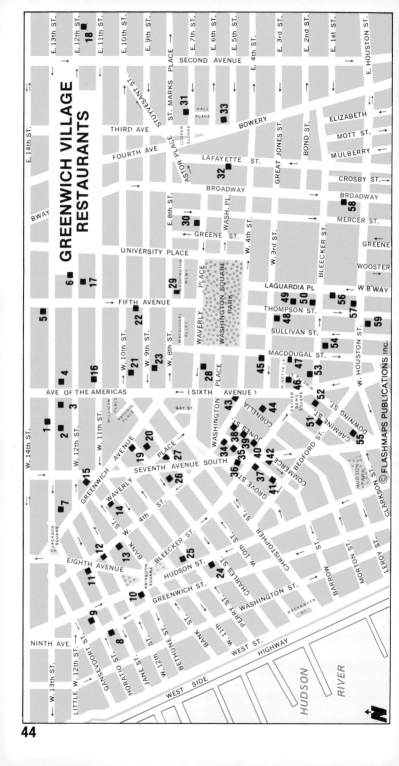

GREENWICH VILLAGE RESTAURANTS

GREENWICH VILLAGE RESTAURANTS — BY MAP NOS.

1 Spain	21 Texarkana	41 Melrose
2 Zinno	22 24 Fifth	42 Manhattan Chili Co
3 La Tulipe	23 Bondini's	43 Tio Pepe
4 La Gauloise	24 Village Green	44 Sabor
5 Sofi's	25 Janice's Fish Place	45 Visiones
6 Asti	26 Sevilla	46 La Boheme
7 Cafe de Bruxelles	27 John Clancy	47 Provence/Minetta
8 El Faro	27 La Metaire	48 Il Mulino
9 Astray Cafe	28 Coach House	49 Livorno
10 La Ripaille	29 One Fifth	50 Grand Ticino
11 Jane St Sfd	30 Garvin's	50 Rincon de Espana
12 Beatrice Inn	31 McSorley's	51 Mary's
13 La Chaumiere	32 Indochine	52 Cent'Anni
14 Ye Waverly Inn	33 Hisae's Place	53 Da Silvano
15 Elephant & Castle	34 Riviera Cafe	54 Le Figaro
16 Gene's	35 One If By Land	55 Urbino
17 Gotham Bar/Grill	36 Il Bufalo	56 Ennio & Michael
18 John's	37 Mitali West	57 Arturo's
19 Angelina's	38 Bianchi & Margherita	58 Bar Lui
20 El Charro	39 Sandolino's/Vanessa	59 Monsoon

GREENWICH VILLAGE RESTAURANTS — ALPHABETICAL

Restaurant	Address	Map No	Cuisine	Avg Price ★	Telephone
Angelina's	41 Greenwich	19	Italian	$10-15	929-1255
Arturo's	106 W Houston	57	Italian	15-20	677-3820
Asti	13 E 12th	6	Italian	25-35	255-9095
Astray Cafe	59 Horatio	9	American	15-20	741-7030
Bar Lui	625 Broadway	58	Italian	15-18	473-8787
Beatrice Inn	285 W 12th	12	Italian	20-24	929-6165
Bianchi & Margherita	186 W 4th	38	Italian	15-25	242-2756
Bondini's	62 W 9th	23	N. Italian	25-32	777-0670
Cafe de Bruxelles	118 Greenwich Ave	7	Fr/Belgium	22-26	206-1830
Cent'Anni	50 Carmine St	52	Italian	35-40	989-9494
Coach House	110 Waverly Pl	28	American	30-40	777-0303
Da Silvano	260 Ave Americas	53	N. Italian	25-35	982-2343
El Charro	4 Charles	20	Mex/Spain	10-14	242-9547
El Faro	823 Greenwich	8	Spanish	15-25	242-9566
Elephant & Castle	68 Greenwich	15	American	12-15	243-1400
Ennio & Michael	504 La Guardia Pl	56	Italian	25-35	677-8577
Garvins	19 Waverly Pl	30	Amer/Contl	25-35	473-5261
Gene's	73 W 11th	16	Ital/Contl	15-21	675-2048
Gotham Bar & Grill	12 E 12th St	17	Amer/Fr	50-60	620-4020
Grand Ticino	228 Thompson	50	Italian	15-20	777-5922
Hisae's Place	35 Cooper Sq	33	Sfd/Orientl	12-17	228-6886
Il Bufalo	87 Seventh Ave	36	Italian	30-35	243-8000
Il Mulino	86 W 3rd St	48	N. Italian	40-50	673-3783
Indochine	430 Lafayette	32	Viet/Camb	25-30	505-5111
Jane Street Sfd Cafe	31 Eighth Ave	11	Seafood	20-25	243-9237
Janice's Fish Place	570 Hudson	25	Seafood	15-25	243-4212
John Clancy's	181 W 10th	27	Seafood	40 +	242-7350
John's	302 E 12th	18	N. Italian	15-20	475-9531
La Boheme	24 Minetta Ln	46	French	20-25	473-6447
La Chaumiere	310 W 4th St	13	French	15-25	741-3374
La Gauloise	502 Ave Americas	4	French	29-32	691-1363
La Metairie	189 W 10th St	27	French	35-40	989-0343
La Ripaille	605 Hudson	10	French	30-35	255-4406
La Tulipe	104 W 13th	3	French	59.00	691-8860
Le Figaro	186 Bleecker	54	American	9-12	677-1100

★ Prices do not include drinks or gratuities

GREENWICH VILLAGE RESTAURANTS (Continued)

Restaurant	Address	Map No	Cuisine	Avg Price ★	Telephone
Livorno	216 Thompson	49	Italian	$15-20	260-1972
Manhattan Chili Co	302 Bleecker St	42	South West	15-20	206-7163
Mary's	42 Bedford	51	Italian	15-25	741-3387
McSorley's	15 E 7th	31	American	8-12	473-9148
Melrose	48 Barrow St	41	New Amer	45-50	691-6800
Minetta Tavern	113 Macdougal	47	Italian	20-25	475-3850
Mitali West	296 Bleecker St	37	Indian	18-22	989-1367
Monsoon	128 W Houston	59	Vietnam	15-20	674-4080
One Fifth	1 Fifth Ave	29	Steak	15-25	260-3434
One If By Land	17 Barrow	35	Amer/Contl	30-40	228-0822
Provence	38 Macdougal St	47	French	22-26	475-7500
Rincon de Espana	226 Thompson	50	Spanish	15-20	475-9891
Riviera Cafe	225 W 4th St	34	Mex/Amer	20-25	242-8732
Sabor	20 Cornelia	44	Cuban	15-25	243-9579
Sandolino's	9 Jones	39	American	8-15	255-6669
Sevilla	62 Charles	26	Spanish	15-25	929-3189
Sofi's	102 Fifth Ave	5	Mediter/Amer	50-55	463-8888
Spain	113 W 13th	1	Spanish	12-18	929-9580
Texarkana	64 W 10th	21	American	25-30	254-5800
Tio Pepe	168 W 4th	43	Spanish	10-15	242-9338
24 Fifth	24 Fifth Ave	22	American	25-30	475-0880
Urbino	78 Carmine St	55	Italian	20-30	242-2676
Vanessa	289 Bleecker	40	Continental	45+	243-4225
Village Green	531 Hudson St	24	New Classic	35-40	255-1650
Visiones	125 Macdougal St	45	Spanish	18-22	473-8842
Ye Waverly Inn	16 Bank	14	American	15-20	243-9396
Zinno	124 W 13th	2	Italian	35-40	924-5182

★ Prices do not include drinks or gratuities

OFF BROADWAY THEATERS (Not in Greenwich Village)

Theater	Address	Type	Telephone
Actors & Directors	412 W 42nd	Experimental workshops	695-5429
Apollo Theater	253 W 125th St	A theatrical landmark	749-5838
Beacon Theater	2124 Broadway	Revivals, musicals, revues	496-7070
Chelsea Playhouse	519 W 23rd	Actors' workshop	243-0992
Delacorte	Central Pk at 81	Shakespearean plays	861-7277
Douglas Fairbanks	432 W 42nd	Varied productions	239-4321
18th St Playhouse	145 W 18th	Drama comdy mime musicl	243-8643
Gramercy Arts	138 E 27th	Rep Co drama cmdy music	889-2850
Harold Clurman	412 W 42nd	Experimental	594-2370
Henry St Settlement	466 Grand	Dramatic workshop	598-0400
Hudson Guild	441 W 26th	Varied productions	760-9810
Improvisation	358 W 44th	Comedy sketches	765-8268
Joyce Theater	175 Eighth Ave	Varied productions	242-0800
Manhattan Thea Club	131 W 55th	Repertory	246-8989
Off Center	436 W 18th	Experimental	929-8299
Open Space	45 St Marks Pl	Avant garde	254-8630
Performing Garage	33-35 Wooster	Experimental repertory	966-3651
Playhouse 91	316 E 91st	Light Opera of Manhattan	831-2000
Playwrights Horizons	406 W 42nd	Drama, revivals	279-4200
Roundabout Theatre	100 E 17th	Repertory	420-1883
SoHo Repertory	80 Varick	Revivals repertory	925-2588
Symphony Space	2537 B'way	Concerts, variety	864-5400
Theatre for New City	155 1st Ave	Varied productions	254-1109
Theater East	211 E 60th	Drama, musicals	838-0177
Theater Four	424 W 55th	Negro Ensemble Co	246-8545
UBU Repertory	149 Mercer St	Readings transl Fr plays	925-0999
Westside Arts	407 W 43rd	Drama comedy	541-8394

1	I Tre Merli
2	Ballato's
3	Raoul's
4	Mezzogiorno
5	Current
6	Greene St
7	Berry's
8	Spring Street
9	Broome St Bar
10	Chanterelle
11	Grotta Azzurra
12	Ruggero's
13	Taormina
14	Ristorante SPQR
15	Angelo of Mulberry
16	Ferrara's
17	Montrachet
18	Barocco
19	Hunan House
20	Hee Seung Fung
21	Phoenix Garden
22	Giambone
23	Antica Roma
24	Mandarin Inn Pell
25	Bo Bo
26	Peking Duck
27	Mandarin Inn
28	Say Eng Look
29	Szechuan Cuisine
30	Odeon

RESTAURANTS—CHINATOWN, LITTLE ITALY, SOHO

Restaurant	Address	Map No.	Cuisine	Average Price ★	Telephone
Angelo of Mulberry	146 Mulberry St	15	Italian	$25-35	966-1277
Antica Roma	40 Mulberry St	23	Italian	20-25	267-2242
Ballato's	55 E Houston	2	N. Italian	25-35	226-9683
Barocco	301 Church St	18	Italian	25-40	431-1445
Berry's	180 Spring St	7	Continental	15-25	226-4394
Bo Bo	20½ Pell St	25	Chinese	10-15	267-8373
Broome St Bar	363 W Broadway	9	American	10-12	925-2086
Chanterelle	89 Grand St	10	French	65.00	966-6960
Current	171 Spring St	5	Seafood	20-25	966-0963
Ferrara's	195 Grand St	16	Pastries	6-8	226-6150
Giambone	42 Mulberry St	22	Italian	15-20	285-1277
Greene Street Cafe	101 Greene St	6	Fr/Amer	25-35	925-2415
Grotta Azzurra	387 Broome St	11	Italian	15-25	925-8775
Hee Seung Fung	46 Bowery	20	Chinese	8-14	374-1319
Hunan House	45 Mott St	19	Chinese	10-15	962-0010
I Tre Merli	463 W B'way	1	Italian	25-35	254-8699
Mandarin Inn	14 Mott St	27	Chinese	10-15	962-5830
Mandarin Inn Pell	34 Pell St	24	Chinese	8-14	267-2092
Mezzogiorno	195 Spring St	4	N. Italian	35-40	334-2112
Montrachet	239 W Broadway	17	French	40-45	219-2777
Odeon	145 W Broadway	30	Nvlle Fr	28-30	233-0507
Peking Duck	22 Mott St	26	Peking	15-25	962-8208
Phoenix Garden	46 Bowery	21	Chinese	10-15	233-6017
Raoul's	180 Prince St	3	French	45+	966-3518
Ristorante SPQR	133 Mulberry St	14	Italian	30-45	925-3120
Ruggero	194 Grand St	12	Italian	25-35	925-1340
Say Eng Look	5 E Broadway	28	Chinese	10-15	732-0796
Spring Street	62 Spring St	8	Natural Fd	10-15	966-0290
Szechuan Cuisine	30 E Broadway	29	Chinese	10-14	966-2326
Taormina	147 Mulberry	13	Italian	30-35	219-1007

★ Prices do not include drinks or gratuities

47

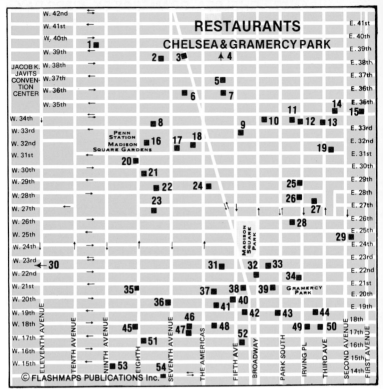

RESTAURANTS
CHELSEA & GRAMERCY PARK

RESTAURANTS—BY MAP NUMBERS

1 Giordano
2 Lou Siegel
3 Club 1407
4 Lavin's
5 Hideaway
6 Lino's
7 Keens
8 Toots Shor
9 Hunan Fifth
10 Salta in Bocca
11 Il Galletto
12 Dolphin
13 Back Porch
14 Nicola Paone
15 El Parador
16 Charley O's
17 Paddy's
18 Dino Casini's

19 Marchi's
20 San Remo
21 Estoril Sol
22 Ballroom
23 Kaspar's
24 Pamplona
25 Savant
26 La Petite Auberge
27 Balkan Armenian
28 La Colombe d'Or
29 Ole
30 Riveranda/Empress
31 Lola's
32 Rascals
33 Pesca
34 Le Parc
35 Onini
36 Claires

37 Periyali
38 Nanou
39 Positano
40 Twenty-Twenty
41 Singalong
42 America
43 Canastel's
44 Cafe du Parc
45 Rogers & Barbero
46 Harvey's Chelsea
47 Da Umberto
48 Il Palazzo
49 Sal Anthony's
50 Tuesday's
51 Chelsea Trattoria
52 Union Square Cafe
53 Old Homestead
54 Quatorze

RESTAURANTS WITH A VIEW

Restaurant	Address	Info page	Restaurant	Address	Info page
Cellar in Sky	World Trade Ctr	33	**The View**	Marriott Mrquis	33
Nirvana Club 1	1 Times Square	33	**Top of Sixes**	666 Fifth Ave	25
Rainbow Room	30 Rockefeller	25	**Windows Wrld**	World Trade Ctr	33
Rivernda/Empr	Pier 62	49	**Wine Bistro**	Novotel Hotel	33
Terrace, The	Columbia Univ	33	**Top of the Park**	Gulf Western	26

48

RESTAURANTS—CHELSEA, GRAMERCY PK, KIPPS BAY

Restaurant	Address	Map No.	Cuisine	Average Price ★	Telephone
America	9 E 18th Street	42	American	$20-30	505-2110
Back Porch, The	488 Third Avenue	13	Continental	20-30	685-3828
Balkan Armenian	129 E 27th Street	27	Armenian	12-15	689-7925
Ballroom	253 W 28th St	22	Span/Contl	25-35	244-3005
Cafe du Parc	106 E 19th Street	44	French	25-35	777-7840
Canastel's	229 Park Ave S	43	N. Italian	55-60	677-9622
Charley O's	Madison Sq Garden	16	Irish Amer	15-25	947-0222
Chelsea Trattoria Ital.	108 Eighth Ave	51	Italian	20-25	924-7786
Claires	156 Seventh Ave	36	Seafood	25-35	255-1955
Club 1407	1407 Broadway	3	American	15-25	575-1407
Da Umberto	107 W 17th St	47	N. Italian	25-30	989-0303
Dino Casini's	132 W 32nd Street	18	Ital/Contl	15-18	695-7995
Dolphin	227 Lexington	12	Seafood	25-30	689-3010
El Parador	325 E 34th Street	15	Mexican	20-25	679-6812
Estoril Sol	382 Eighth Ave	21	Portuguese	18-22	947-1043
Giordano	409 W 39th Street	1	Italian	25-30	947-9811
Harvey's Chelsea	108 W 18th Street	46	American	15-25	243-5644
Hideaway	32 W 37th Street	5	Amer/Ital	20-25	947-8940
Hunan Fifth Ave	323 Fifth Ave	9	Chinese	12-20	686-3366
Il Galletto	120 E 34th Street	11	Italian	20-25	889-1990
Il Palazzo	18 W 18th Street	48	N. Italian	30-35	924-3800
Kaspar's	250 W 27th Street	23	Continental	20-30	989-3804
Keens	72 W 36th Street	7	American	50-55	947-3636
La Colombe d'Or	134 E 26th Street	28	French	20-30	689-0666
La Petite Auberge	116 Lexington	26	French	20-30	689-5003
Lavin's	23 W 39th St	4	American	40-45	921-1288
Le Parc	Gramery Pk Hotel	34	Continental	20-28	475-4320
Lino's	147 W 36th Street	6	N. Italian	20-35	695-6444
Lola's	30 W 22nd St	31	Amer/Carib	30-35	675-6700
Lou G. Siegel	209 W 38th Street	2	Kosher	18-27	921-4433
Marchi's	251 E 31 Street	19	Italian	26.50	679-2494
Nanou	24 E 21st Street	38	Fr/Mediter	30-35	505-5252
Nicola Paone	207 E 34th Street	14	Italian	60-65	889-3239
Old Homestead	56 Ninth Avenue	53	American	16-28	242-9040
Ole	434 Second Ave	29	Spanish	15-20	725-1953
Onini	217 Eighth Avenue	35	Italian	20-25	243-6446
Paddy's Clam House	367 Seventh Ave	17	Seafood	15-25	244-1040
Pamplona	822 Sixth Avenue	24	Spanish	15-25	683-4242
Periyali	35 W 20th St	37	Greek	20-30	463-7890
Pesca	23 E 22nd St	33	Seafood	30-35	533-2293
Positano	250 Park Ave S	39	N. Italian	30-35	777-6211
Quatorze	240 W 14th Street	54	French	25-35	206-7006
Rascals	12 E 22nd St	32	American	15-20	420-1777
Riveranda/Empress NY	Pier 62 & Hudson	30	Continental	55-65	929-8540
Rogers & Barbero	149 Eighth Ave	45	American	20-30	243-2020
Sal Anthony's	55 Irving Place	49	Italian	20-30	982-9030
Salta in Bocca	179 Madison Ave	10	Italian	35-40	684-1757
San Remo	393 Eighth Ave	20	N. Italian	25-30	564-1819
Savant	132 Lexington	25	Cajun	20-30	686-3959
Singalong	17 W 19th Street	41	American	10-18	206-8660
Toots Shor	233 W 33rd Street	8	American	30-35	279-8150
Tuesday's	190 Third Avenue	50	American	10-15	533-7900
Twenty-Twenty	20 W 20th St	40	Fr/Amer	25-30	627-1444
Union Square Cafe	21 E 16th Street	52	Ital/French	25-30	243-4020

★ Prices do not include drinks or gratuities

49

MADISON AVENUE SHOPS

Map (72ND Street to 60TH Street, along Madison Avenue):

- 72ND
- CACHE CACHE 1
- LASSERRE 2
- 3 POLO/ RALPH LAUREN
- 71ST
- PIERRE DEUX 4
- 6 ST LAURENT RIVE GAUCHE
- MATSUDA 5
- 70TH
- CARTIER 7
- MISSONI 8
- 9 MADISON BOOKSHOP
- 10 LANVIN
- 11 PRATESI
- 69TH
- KENZO 12
- JAEGER 13
- GIANNI VERSACE 14
- 15 VALENTINO
- 16 SIR DAVID
- 17 VENEZIANO
- 18 G. ARMANI
- 19 PERRIS
- 68TH
- TAHARI 20
- VERI UOMO 21
- BALOGH 22
- 23 CERUTTI KRIZIA
- 24 E UNGARO
- 25 D. CENCI
- 26 PIERRE BALMAIN
- 67TH
- S RYKIEL 27
- THAXTON 28
- N BEACH 29
- 30 CIRO
- 31 MONTENA-POLEONE
- 32 FRED LEIGHTON
- 66TH
- 33 CHARLES JOURDAN
- 34 TENNIS LADY/MAN
- 65TH
- ANDREA CARRANO 35
- DANA COTE D'AZUR 36
- BETSY BUNKY NINI 37
- 38 WALTER STEIGER
- 39 MANFREDI
- 64TH
- LAURA ASHLEY 40
- COACH 41
- 42 DIANE B
- 43 LA BAGAGE
- 44 SPREI FRER
- 45 BRAUN
- 46 DES CHAMPS
- 47 LOEWE
- 63RD
- LANCEL 48
- 49 FURLA
- 50 T. CRISCI
- 51 AVENUE MONTAIGNE
- 52 THE LIMITED
- 62ND
- CHRISTOFLE 53
- PERRY ELLIS SHOES 54
- LALIQUE 55
- 56 BALLY
- 57 JULIE
- 58 G. JENSEN
- 59 SHERRY LEHMANN
- 61ST
- 60TH

MADISON AVENUE

© FLASHMAPS PUBLICATIONS Inc.

50

Shop	Map No.	Telephone
Andrea Carrano	35	570-9020
Ave Montaigne	51	935-9455
Bally of Switzerland	56	751-3540
Balogh Jewels	22	517-9440
Betsey Bunkey Nini	37	744-6716
Braun, E & Co.	45	838-0650
Cache Cache Ltd.	1	744-6886
Cartier	7	685-0006
Cenci, D	25	628-5910
Cerutti	23	737-7540
Charles Jourdan	33	628-0133
Christofle	53	308-9390
Ciro	30	628-1290
Coach Store	41	319-1772
Dana Cote d'Azur	36	249-1300
Des Champs	46	355-2522
Diane, B	42	759-0988
Fred Leighton	32	288-1872
Furla	49	755-8986
Georg Jensen	58	759-6457
Gianni Versace	14	744-5572
Giorgio Armani	18	988-9191
Jaeger Internat'l	13	628-3350
Julie	57	688-2345
Kenzo-Paris	12	737-8640
Krizia	23	628-8180
La Bagagerie	43	758-6570
Lalique	55	355-6550
Lancel Leather	48	753-6918
Lanvin	10	472-9436
Lasserre	2	734-5555
Laura Ashley	40	735-5000
Limited, The	52	838-8787
Loewe	47	308-7700
Madison Ave Books	9	535-6130
Manfredi	39	734-8710
Matsuda	5	988-9514
Missoni	8	517-9339
Montenapoleone	31	535-2660
North Beach Leather	29	772-0707
Perris, Bernard	19	288-9800
Perry Ellis Shoes	54	980-7011
Pierre Balmain	26	628-4260
Pierre Deux	4	570-9343
Polo/Ralph Lauren	3	606-2100
Pratesi	11	288-2315
Rykiel, Sonia	27	744-0880
St Laurent/RiveGauche	6	988-3821
Sherry-Lehmann	59	838-7500
Sir David	16	737-2422
Sprei Freres	44	838-4240
Tahari	20	535-1515
Tanino Crisci	50	308-7778
Tennis Lady	34	535-8601
Thaxton & Co	28	988-4001
Ungaro, Emanuel	24	249-4090
Valentino	15	772-6969
Veneziano	17	988-0211
Veri Uomo	21	737-9200
Walter Steiger	38	570-1212

Map (Fifth Avenue)

```
58TH →
BERGDORF GOODMAN 1        3  F.A.O. SCHWARZ
VAN CLEEF ARPELS 2        4  MORANO'S
                          5  LERON
57TH ←→
I MILLER JAEGERS 8        12 TIFFANY
FERRAGAMO'S 9             13 TRUMP TOWER
DOUBLEDAY 10
HALLMARK 11
56TH ←
WINSTON 14                16 FERRAGAMO STEUBEN
PRESBYTERIAN CHURCH       17 BELTRANI
                          18 EVYAN/CIRO
55TH ←                    19 BALLY
                          20 N SHERMAN
GOTHAM BLDG               22 FRED J
                          23 GODIVA
                          24 BIJAN
                          25 WEMPE
                          26 ELIZ ARDEN
54TH →                    27 GUCCI
ACQUA-SCUTUM 28           29 GUCCI
ST. THOMAS CHURCH         30 FORTUNOFF
53RD ←                    32 CARRANO
BENETTON 34               33 DOUBLEDAY
BOTTICELLI 35
B. DALTON 36
52ND →
PIAGET BLDG               38 CARTIER
                          39 MARK CROSS
                          40 H STERN
                          41 MARIO VALENTINO
51ST ←
ROCKEFELLER CENTER        ST PATRICKS CATHEDRAL
50TH →
DUNHILL 42
CUSTOM SHP 43
BOTTICELLI 44             45 SAKS FIFTH AVE
PIERRE D'ALBY 45
49TH ←
MIKIMOTO 47
BARNES & NOBLE 48         49 SCRIBNER'S
48TH →
47TH ←
INTERNAT'L JEWELERS 50    51 FRED THE FURRIER
46TH →                    52 RODIER
                          53 575 FIFTH AVE CENTER
```

AVENUE / FIFTH

© FLASHMAPS PUBLICATIONS Inc.

FIFTH AVENUE SHOPS

Shop	Map No.	Telephone
Acquascutum	28	975-0250
Bally	19	751-9082
Barnes & Noble	48	765-0590
Beltrani	17	838-4101
Benetton	34	399-9860
Bergdorf Goodman	1	753-7300
Bijan	24	758-7500
Botticelli	35	582-2984
Botticelli	44	582-6313
Carrano	32	752-6111
Cartier	38	753-0111
Chandler Shoes	25	688-2140
Ciro	18	752-0441
Custom Shop	43	245-2499
Dalton, Books	36	247-1740
Doubleday Books	10	397-0550
Doubleday Books	33	223-6550
Dunhill	42	489-5580
Elizabeth Arden	26	407-7900
Evyan	18	752-0725
Ferragamo's	16	759-3822
Ferragamo's	9	246-6211
575 Fifth Ave Center	53	986-4676
Fortunoff	30	758-6660
Fred Joaillier	22	832-3733
Fred the Furrier	51	765-3877
Godiva	23	593-2845
Gucci	27	826-2600
Gucci	29	826-2600
Hallmark Gallery	8	489-8320
I. Miller	50	581-0062
International Jewelers	8	869-8600
Jaegers	5	753-0370
Leron	39	753-6700
Mark Cross	47	421-3000
Mikimoto	4	586-6992
Morano's	20	751-7750
Nat Sherman	45	751-9100
Pierre d'Alby	52	541-7110
Rodier	46	599-2495
Saks Fifth Ave	3	753-4000
Schwarz, FAO	49	644-9443
Scribner's Books	40	758-9797
Stern, H	16	688-0300
Steuben Glass	12	752-1441
Tiffany	41	755-8000
Valentino, Mario	2	319-7756
Van Cleef & Arpels	25	644-9500
Wempe	14	751-4884
Winston, Harry	13	245-2000

Trump Tower Shops:

Abrcrmble	832-1001	Cartier	308-0840
Asprey	688-1811	Lina Lee	556-2678
Buccellati	308-5533	Lingerie	980-8811
C Jourdan	644-3830	Martha	826-8855
Cashmere	758-7621	Sports B.	319-7711

OTHER MAJOR STORES PAGE 52

OTHER MAJOR STORES & CENTERS

B. Altman	Fifth Ave at 34th Street	689-7000
Barney's	106 Seventh Ave at 17th St	929-9000
Bendel, Henri	10 W 57th Street	247-1100
Bloomingdales	1000 Third Ave at 59th St	355-5900
Bonwit Tellers	4-10 E 57th Street	593-3333
Brooks Brothers	346 Madison Ave at 44th St	682-8800
Georg Jensen	683 Madison Avenue	759-6457
Hammacher Schlemmer	147 E 57th-betw Lexington&Third	421-9000
Herald Center	Broadway at 34th (**8 floors**)	714-2530
Lord & Taylor	Fifth Ave & 38th Street	391-3344
Macy's	Broadway & 34th St-Herald Square	971-6000
Market at Citicorp Center	Lexington & 53rd St (**13 shops**)	559-2319
Place des Antiquaires	125 E 57th St (**75 shops**)	758-2900
South Street Seaport	Front & Water St (**20 shops**)	732-7678
Strand Bookstore	828 Broadway at 12th St	473-1452
Tower Records	692 Broadway at 4th St	505-1500
Trump Tower	Fifth Ave & 56th (**40 shops**)	832-2000
World Trade Concourse	1 World Trade Center (60 shops)	466-4170

GLOSSARY

	French	German	Italian	Spanish	Russian
Architecture	Architecture	Architektur	Architettura	Arquitectura	Архитектура
Art	Art	Kunst	Arte	Arte	Искусство
Buses	Autobus	Autobusse	Autobus	Autobús	Автóбусы
Churches	Églises	Kirchen	Chiese	Iglesias	Церкви
Colleges	Universités	Universitäten	Università	Universidades	Университеты
Embassies	Ambassades	Botschaften	Ambasciate	Embajadas	Посольства
Emergency Numbers	Numéros d'urgence	Notnummern	Numeri d'emergenza		Телефоны скорой
Galleries	Galléries	Gallerien	Galleria	Galería	Галлереи
History	Histoire	Geschichte	Storia	Istoria	История
Highways	Grandes Routes	Landstrassen	Autostrade	Carreteras	Дороги
Hospitals	Hopîtaux	Krankenhäuser	Ospedali	hospital	Больницы
Hotels	Hôtels	Hotels	Hotel	Hotel	Гостиницы
Libraries	Bibliotèques	Bibliotheken	Biblioteche	Bibliotecas	Биóлиотеки
Museums	Musées	Museen	Musei	Museos	Музеи
Music	Musique	Musik	Musica	Musica	Музыка
Movies	Cinémas	Filme	Cinema	Películas	Кино
Parks	Parcs	Parks	Giardini Publici	Parques	Парки
Restaurants	Restaurants	Restaurants	Ristoranti	Restaurantes	Рестораны
Science	Science	Wissenschaft	Scienza	Ciencia	Наука
Shops	Grands Magasins	Einkaufen	Negozi	Negocios	Покупки— *Магазипы*
Sports	Sports	Sport	Sport	Desportes	спорт
Subways	Métro	Untergrundbahnen	Metropolitana	Subterráneo	Метро
Taxi	Taxi	Taxi	Tassì	Taxi	Такси
Theaters	Théâtres	Theater	Teatri	Teatros	Театры
Zoo	Zoo	Zoo	Giardino Zoologico	Jardín Zoológico	Зоологический

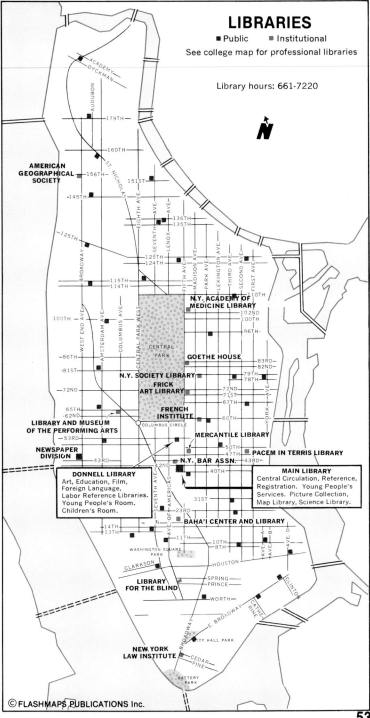

LIBRARIES

■ Public ■ Institutional

See college map for professional libraries

Library hours: 661-7220

N

ACADEMY
DYCKMAN

179TH

160TH

**AMERICAN
GEOGRAPHICAL
SOCIETY**
156TH   151ST

145TH

136TH
135TH

125TH
124TH

115TH
114TH

**N.Y. ACADEMY OF
MEDICINE LIBRARY**
102ND
100TH
96TH

CENTRAL
PARK

86TH
81ST   83RD
             82ND
GOETHE HOUSE
79TH
78TH
N.Y. SOCIETY LIBRARY
72ND
**FRICK   71ST
ART LIBRARY**   67TH
             60TH
**FRENCH
INSTITUTE**
COLUMBUS CIRCLE

65TH
62ND

**LIBRARY AND MUSEUM
OF THE PERFORMING ARTS**
53RD

MERCANTILE LIBRARY
50TH
47TH ■ **PACEM IN TERRIS LIBRARY**
43RD
**NEWSPAPER
DIVISION** 43RD
N.Y. BAR ASSN.
40TH

DONNELL LIBRARY
Art, Education, Film,
Foreign Language,
Labor Reference Libraries.
Young People's Room.
Children's Room.

MAIN LIBRARY
Central Circulation, Reference,
Registration. Young People's
Services. Picture Collection,
Map Library, Science Library.

31ST

23RD

BAHA'I CENTER AND LIBRARY
14TH
13TH   10TH
             8TH

WASHINGTON SQUARE
PARK
CLARKSON   HOUSTON

**LIBRARY
FOR THE BLIND**
SPRING
PRINCE

WORTH

E. BROADWAY

CITY HALL PARK

**NEW YORK
LAW INSTITUTE**
CEDAR
PINE

BATTERY
PARK

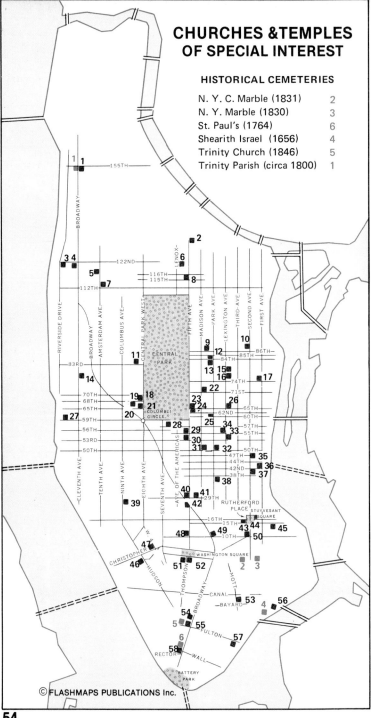

CHURCHES & TEMPLES
OF SPECIAL INTEREST

HISTORICAL CEMETERIES

N. Y. C. Marble (1831)	2
N. Y. Marble (1830)	3
St. Paul's (1764)	6
Shearith Israel (1656)	4
Trinity Church (1846)	5
Trinity Parish (circa 1800)	1

© FLASHMAPS PUBLICATIONS Inc.

54

CHURCHES & TEMPLES OF SPECIAL INTEREST

(In Manhattan there are over 1200 houses of worship, representing 100 denominations)

1 Church Intercession	20 Stephen Wise Syn	39 Church Holy Apostles
2 St. Andrew's	21 Holy Trinity	40 Marble Collegiate
3 Riverside	22 St. James Episcopal	41 Ltle Church Arnd Cor
4 Union Theological	23 Temple Emanu-El	42 Cathedral St. Sava
5 St. Paul's Chapel	24 Fifth Av Synagogue	43 Friends Meeting Hse
6 St. Martin's	25 Christ Church	44 St. George's
7 St. John the Divine	26 St. Vincent Ferrer	45 Immaculate Conceptn
8 Church of Brethren	27 St. Paul the Apostle	46 St. Luke's Chapel
9 Park Av Synagogue	28 Calvary Baptist	47 St.John's Evangelical
10 Holy Trinity	29 Fifth Av Presbyterian	48 Church of Ascension
11 Congr Rodeph Sholom	30 St. Thomas	49 Grace Church
12 Park Ave Christian	31 St. Patrick's	50 St. Mark's-Bouwerie
13 St. Ignatius Loyola	32 St. Bartholomew's	51 Judson Memorial
14 West End Collegiate	33 St. Peter's	52 Holy Trinity Chapel
15 All Souls Unitarian	34 Central Synagogue	54 St. Peter's
16 St. Jean Baptiste	35 Holy Family	55 St. Paul's Chapel
17 Holy Trinity Greek	36 Church of UN	56 St. James R.C.
18 Spanish Synagogue	37 Church of Covenant	57 John St Methodist
19 Church of LDS	38 Church of Our Savior	58 Trinity Church

CHURCHES & TEMPLES—ALPHABETICAL

Church	Address	Map No.	Telephone
All Souls Unitarian	1157 Lexington Ave	15	535-5530
Calvary Baptist	123 W 57th Street	28	975-0170
Cathedral St. John Divine (Episcopal) ★	Amsterdam & 112th	7	316-7400
Cathedral of St. Sava (Serbian Orthodox)	15 W 25th Street	42	242-9417
Central Synagogue (1870)	652 Lex Ave at 55th	34	838-5122
Christ Church (Methodist)	520 Park Ave	25	838-3036
Church of Ascension (Episcopal)	Fifth Ave & 10th St	48	254-8620
Church of Brethren	27 W 115th Street	8	369-2620
Church of Latter Day Saints (Mormon)	2 Lincoln Square	19	595-1825
Church of Our Savior (Roman Catholic)	59 Park Ave	38	679-8166
Church of the Covenant (Presbyterian)	310 E 42nd Street	37	697-3185
Church of the Intercession (Episcopal)	Broadway & 155th St	1	283-6200
Church of the UN (Non-denominational)	777 U N Plaza	36	661-1762
Congregation Rodeph Sholom	7 W 83rd Street	11	362-8800
Fifth Avenue Presbyterian	Fifth Ave & 55th St	29	247-0490
Fifth Avenue Synagogue	5 E 62nd Street	24	838-2122
Friends Meeting House (1861)	15 Rutherford	43	777-8866
Grace Episcopal (1843)	802 Broadway	49	254-2000
Holy Apostles (Roman Catholic-1840)	296 Ninth Ave	39	807-6799
Holy Family (Roman Catholic)	315 E 47th Street	35	753-3401
Holy Trinity Cathedral (Greek Orthodox)	319 E 74th Street	17	288-3215
Holy Trinity Chapel (Roman Catholic)	Washington Square S	52	674-7236
Holy Trinity (Episcopal-1897)	316 E 88th Street	10	289-4100
Holy Trinity (Lutheran)	Central Pk W & 65th	21	877-6815
Immaculate Conception (Roman Cath.)	414 E 14th Street	45	254-0200
John Street Methodist (1841)	44 John St	57	269-0014
Judson Memorial Baptist (1890)	55 Washington Sq	51	477-0351
Little Church Around the Corner	1 E 29th Street	41	684-6770
Marble Collegiate (1854)	Fifth Ave & 29th St	40	686-2770
Park Avenue Christian	1010 Park Ave	12	288-3246
Park Avenue Synagogue	50 E 87th Street	9	369-2600
Riverside (Non-denominational)	Riverside Dr& 122nd	3	222-5900
Spanish & Portuguese Synagogue	8 W 70th Street	18	873-0300
St. Andrew's (Episcopal-1889)	Fifth Ave & 127th St	2	534-0896
St. Bartholomew's (Episcopal-1917)	109 E 50th Street	32	751-1616

★ *largest Gothic cathedral in the world—10,000 worshippers*

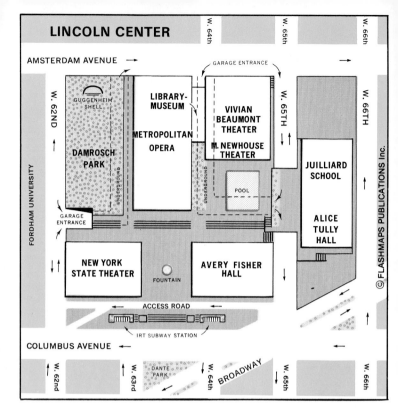

CHURCHES & TEMPLES (Continued)

Church	Address	Map No.	Telephone
St. George's (Episcopal-1846)	209 E 16th Street	44	475-0830
St. Ignatius Loyola (Roman Catholic-1895)	980 Park Ave	13	288-3588
St. James (Episcopal)	865 Madison Ave	22	288-4100
St. James (Roman Catholic)	23 Oliver	56	233-0161
St. Jean Baptiste (Roman Catholic-1910)	184 E 76th Street	16	288-5082
St. John's Lutheran	81 Christopher St	47	242-5737
St. Luke's Chapel (Episcopal)	487 Hudson St	46	924-0562
St. Mark's in the Bowery (Episc-1799)	Second Ave & 10th	50	674-6377
St. Martin's Episcopal (1887)	230 Lenox Ave	6	534-4531
St. Patrick's Cathedral (Catholic-1858)	Fifth Ave & 50th	31	753-2261
St. Paul the Apostle (Roman Catholic)	415 W 59th Street	27	265-3209
St. Paul's Chapel at Columbia (1904)	Broadway & 116th	5	534-4422
St. Paul's Chapel (Episcopal-1764) ★	Broadway & Fulton	55	602-0874
St. Peter's (Lutheran-1977)	619 Lexington Ave	33	935-2200
St. Peter's (Roman Catholic-1836)	16 Barclay St	54	233-8355
St. Thomas (Episcopal-1909)	Fifth Ave & 53rd	30	757-7013
St. Vincent Ferrer (Roman Catholic-1918)	Lexington & 66th	26	744-2080
Stephen Wise Free Synagogue	30 W 68th Street	20	877-4050
Temple Emanu-El (1930)	1 E 65th Street	23	744-1400
Trinity (Episcopal-1846)	74 Trinity Place	58	602-0800
Union Theological Brown Mem Chapel	Broadway & 120th	4	662-7100
West End Collegiate (1892)	West End & 77th	14	787-1566

56   ★ Site of Washington's first Inaugural address

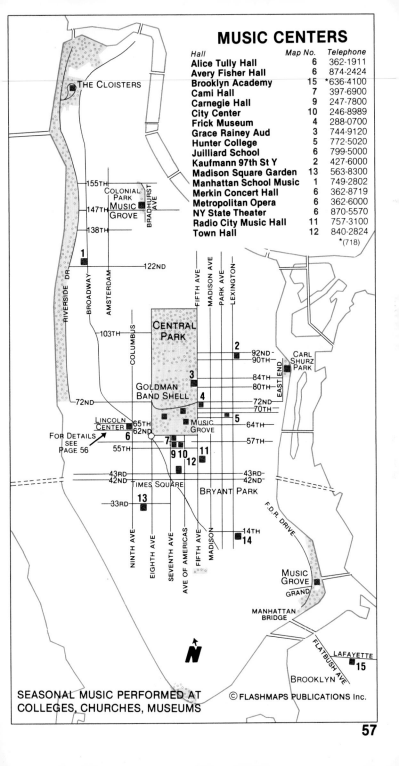

MUSIC CENTERS

Hall	Map No.	Telephone
Alice Tully Hall	6	362-1911
Avery Fisher Hall	6	874-2424
Brooklyn Academy	15	*636-4100
Cami Hall	7	397-6900
Carnegie Hall	9	247-7800
City Center	10	246-8989
Frick Museum	4	288-0700
Grace Rainey Aud	3	744-9120
Hunter College	5	772-5020
Juilliard School	6	799-5000
Kaufmann 97th St Y	2	427-6000
Madison Square Garden	13	563-8300
Manhattan School Music	1	749-2802
Merkin Concert Hall	6	362-8719
Metropolitan Opera	6	362-6000
NY State Theater	6	870-5570
Radio City Music Hall	11	757-3100
Town Hall	12	840-2824
		*(718)

THE CLOISTERS

COLONIAL PARK
MUSIC GROVE

155TH
147TH
138TH
122ND

RIVERSIDE DR
BROADWAY
AMSTERDAM
COLUMBUS
BRADHURST AVE

CENTRAL PARK

GOLDMAN BAND SHELL

LINCOLN CENTER

FOR DETAILS SEE PAGE 56

103RD
72ND
65TH
62ND
55TH

FIFTH AVE
MADISON AVE
PARK AVE
LEXINGTON

92ND
90TH
84TH
80TH
72ND
70TH
64TH
57TH

EAST END

CARL SHURZ PARK

MUSIC GROVE

43RD
42ND
33RD

TIMES SQUARE

BRYANT PARK

F.D.R. DRIVE

NINTH AVE
EIGHTH AVE
SEVENTH AVE
AVE OF AMERICAS
FIFTH AVE
MADISON

14TH

MUSIC GROVE

GRAND

MANHATTAN BRIDGE

FLATBUSH AVE
LAFAYETTE

BROOKLYN

N

SEASONAL MUSIC PERFORMED AT COLLEGES, CHURCHES, MUSEUMS

© FLASHMAPS PUBLICATIONS Inc.

57

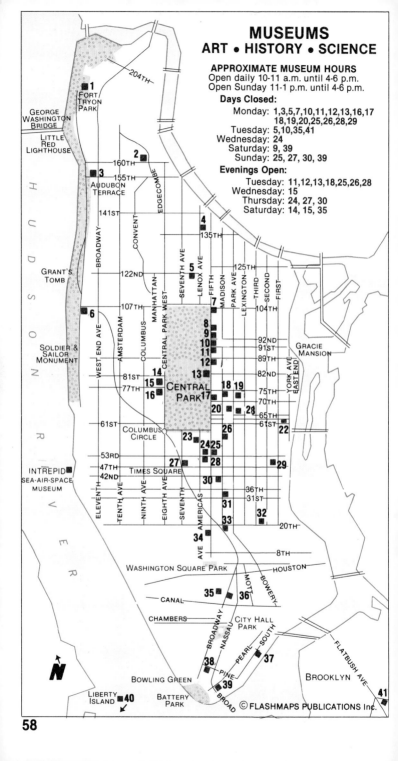

MUSEUMS
ART • HISTORY • SCIENCE

APPROXIMATE MUSEUM HOURS
Open daily 10-11 a.m. until 4-6 p.m.
Open Sunday 11-1 p.m. until 4-6 p.m.

Days Closed:
Monday: 1,3,5,7,10,11,12,13,16,17
18,19,20,25,26,28,29
Tuesday: 5,10,35,41
Wednesday: 24
Saturday: 9, 39
Sunday: 25, 27, 30, 39

Evenings Open:
Tuesday: 11,12,13,18,25,26,28
Wednesday: 15
Thursday: 24, 27, 30
Saturday: 14, 15, 35

© FLASHMAPS PUBLICATIONS Inc.

58

MUSEUMS—BY MAP NUMBERS

1 Cloisters, The	10 Cooper Hewitt	20 Ctr Inter-Amer	31 Morgan Lib
2 Morris-Jumel	11 Natl Ac Design	21 China House	32 Police Acad
3 Amer Aca Arts	12 Guggenheim	22 A Adam Smith	33 Theo Roosvelt
3 Amer Indian	13 Metropolitan	24 Mus Mod Art	34 Forbes Gallery
3 Hispan/Numis	14 Hayden Planet	25 Mus Broadcst	35 New Mus Contp
4 Schomburg	15 Am Natural His	26 AT &T	36 Hispanic Cont
5 Studio Mus	16 NY Historical	27 Whitney Equit	37 So St Seaport
6 Nichls Roerich	17 Frick	28 Amer Craft	38 NY Stock Exch
7 Mus City NY	18 Whitney Amer	29 African-Amer	39 Fraunces Tvrn
8 Intern'l Photo	19 Asia House	29 Japan Society	40 Amer Immigrtn
9 Jewish Mus	20 African Art	30 Whitney PM	41 Brooklyn Mus

MUSEUMS—ALPHABETICAL

Museum	Address	Map No	*(Area 718) Telephone
Abigail Adams Smith House	421 E 61st Street	22	838-6878
African American Institute	833 UN Plaza	29	949-5666
African Art Center	54 E 68th Street	20	861-1200
American Academy of Arts & Letters	633 W 155th Street	3	368-5900
American Craft Museum	40 W 53rd Street	28	956-6047
American Indian Heye Found	Broadway & 155th St	3	283-2497
American Museum of Immigration	Statue of Liberty	36	363-3200
American Museum of Natural History	Central Pk W & 79th	15	769-5100
Asia Society Gallery	Park Ave at 70th Street	19	288-6400
AT & T Infoquest	550 Madison Avenue	26	605-5555
Brooklyn Museum	200 Eastern Pkwy	41	*638-5000
Center for Inter-Amer Relations	680 Park Avenue	20	249-8950
China House	125 E 65th Street	21	744-8181
Cloisters, The	Fort Tryon Park	1	923-3700
Cooper Hewitt/The Smithsonian	2 E 91st Street	10	860-6898
Forbes Magazine Galleries	60 Fifth Avenue	34	206-5548
Fraunces Tavern Museum	54 Pearl Street	39	425-1778
Frick Collection	Fifth Ave & 70th St	17	288-0700
Guggenheim Museum	Fifth Ave & 89th St	12	360-3500
Hayden Planetarium/Laserium	Central Pk W & 80th St	14	769-5920
Hispanic Contemporary	584 Broadway	36	966-6699
Hispanic Society of America	Broadway & 155th St	3	690-0743
Internt'l Center of Photography	1130 Fifth Avenue	8	860-1777
Japan Society	333 E 47th Street	29	832-1155
Jewish Museum	1109 Fifth Ave at 92nd	9	860-1888
Metropolitan Museum of Art	Fifth Ave & 82nd St	13	535-7710
Morgan, Pierpont Library	29 E 36th Street	31	685-0610
Morris-Jumel Mansion	Edgecombe & W 160th	2	923-8008
Museum of Broadcasting	1 E 53rd Street	25	752-7684
Museum of the City of New York	Fifth Ave & 103rd St	7	534-1672
Museum of Modern Art (MOMA)	11 W 53rd Street	24	708-9480
National Academy of Design	1083 Fifth Avenue	11	369-4880
New Museum of Contemporary Art	583 Broadway	35	219-1222
New York Historical Society	170 Central Pk W	16	873-3400
New York Stock Exchange	20 Broadway	38	623-5167
Nicholas Roerich Museum	319 W 107th Street	6	864-7752
Numismatic Society America	Broadway & 156th St	3	234-3130
Police Academy Museum	235 E 20th Street	32	477-9753
Schomburg Black Culture Collection	515 Lenox Avenue	4	862-4000
South Street Seaport Museum	Fulton & South Street	37	669-9424
Studio Museum in Harlem	144 W 125th Street	5	864-4500
Theodore Roosevelt House	28 E 20th Street	33	260-1616
Whitney Museum American Art	Madison Ave& 75th St	18	570-3676
Whitney Museum-Equitable Ctr	787 Seventh Avenue	27	554-1113
Whitney Museum-Philip Morris	120 Park Avenue	30	878-2550

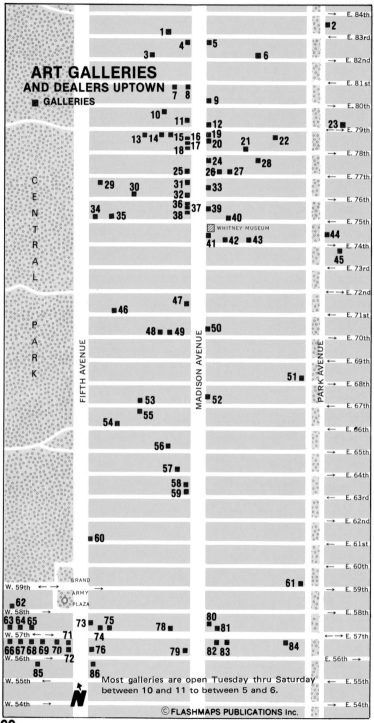

ART GALLERIES
AND DEALERS UPTOWN
■ GALLERIES

CENTRAL PARK

FIFTH AVENUE

MADISON AVENUE

PARK AVENUE

Whitney Museum

GRAND ARMY PLAZA

Most galleries are open Tuesday thru Saturday
between 10 and 11 to between 5 and 6.

E. 84th
E. 83rd
E. 82nd
E. 81st
E. 80th
E. 79th
E. 78th
E. 77th
E. 76th
E. 75th
E. 74th
E. 73rd
E. 72nd
E. 71st
E. 70th
E. 69th
E. 68th
E. 67th
E. 66th
E. 65th
E. 64th
E. 63rd
E. 62nd
E. 61st
E. 60th
W. 59th
E. 59th
W. 58th
E. 58th
W. 57th
E. 57th
W. 56th
E. 56th
W. 55th
E. 55th
W. 54th
E. 54th

N

© FLASHMAPS PUBLICATIONS Inc.

60

ART GALLERIES UPTOWN—BY MAP NUMBERS

1 Byron
2 Schaeffer
3 La Boetie
4 Neil Isman
5 Raydon
6 Kerr, Coe
7 Elkon Robt
8 Gall Schreiner
9 Smith
10 Salander-O'R
11 Johnson, Jay
11 Le Loup
12 Sindin
13 De Rempich
14 Acquavella
15 Rosenberg, Paul
16 Adler, Rachel
   Forum
   Saidenberg
   Wittenborn
17 Perls
18 Graham
19 Kenneth Lux
20 Schweitzer
21 Isselbacher
22 Lafayette Parke
23 Feigen, Richard
24 Findlay, Peter
25 Weintraub
26 Staempfli
28 Spanierman
29 Castelli Uptown
30 Mazoh
31 Aberbach

31 Findlay, David
32 Perlow, Rich
33 Madison Ave
34 Benedek
35 CDS
36 Niveau
37 Safani
38 Childs
38 Jordan/Volpe
39 Davlyn
40 Fourcade
41 Rolly/Michaux
42 Urdang, Bertha
43 Bernard
43 Hutton
44 Chapellier
45 Sportsman's
46 Hamilton, M
46 Kovesday
47 Carus
48 Knoedler
49 Hirschl/Adler
50 Hirschl/Adler
50 Mathes
51 Ctr Inter-Amer
52 Christie Cntmp
53 A.C.A.
53 Adler, A. M.
54 Newhouse
55 Babcock
56 York, Richard
57 Wildenstein
58 Allison, H.V.
59 Vercel, Felix

60 Schiller-W
61 Christie's
62 Dorsky
63 Brewster
   De Nagy, Tibor
   Shippee
64 Protech, Max
65 Hammer
66 Armstrong
   Dintenfass
   Drake, Doug
   Frumkin, Allan
   Heidenberg
   Jacobson
   La Magna
   Schoelkopt
   Sumers, Martin
   Tatistcheff
   Viridian
67 Kennedy
67 Marlborough
68 Gallery 84
69 Arras
   Donson
   Fischbach
   Gal St Etienne
   Goodman, M
   Grand Central
   Multiples
   Reece Gal
   Siegel, Ruth
70 Assoc Amer
   Blum, Helman
   Deutsch, Sid

70 Rosenberg, A
71 Lever Meyersn
72 Borgenicht
   Gimpel & W
   Kraushaar
   Solomon
   Zabriskie
73 Berry/Hill
74 Fitch-Febvrel
75 Drey, Paul
   Dyansen
   Midtown
76 Amazoni Art
   Circle
78 Wally Findlay
79 IBM Gallery
80 Ronin
81 Caro, Frank
   Del Re, Marisa
   Emmerich
   Findlay, D, Jr
   Goodman, Jas
   Kent Fine Arts
   Matisse, Pierre
   McKee, David
   Miller, Robert
   Washburn
   Zarre, Andre
82 Pace
82 Rosenberg&S
83 Pearl, Marilyn
84 Orrefors
85 Eric
86 Steuben

ART GALLERIES UPTOWN—ALPHABETICAL

Gallery	Address	Map No	Gallery	Address	Map No
Aberbach	988 Madison	31	Caro, Frank	41 E 57th	81
A.C.A.	21 E 67th	53	Carus	872 Madison	47
Acquavella	18 E 79th	14	Castelli Uptown	4 E 77th	29
Adler, A M	21 E 67th	53	CDS	13 E 75th	35
Adler, Rachel	1018 Madison	16	Ctr Inter-Amer	680 Park Ave	51
Allison, H. V.	716 Madison	58	Chapellier	815 Park Ave	44
Amazoni Art	725 Fifth	76	Childs	956 Madison	38
Armstrong	50 W 57th	66	Christie Contemp	799 Madison	52
Arras	24 W 57th	69	Christie's	502 Park Ave	61
Assoc.Amer.Art.	20 W 57th	70	Christie's East	219 E 67th	★
Babcock	20 E 67th	55	Circle	725 Fifth Ave	76
Benedek	3 E 75th	34	Cole, Sylvan	200 W 57th	★
Bernard Claude	33 E 74th	43	Cordier/Ekstrom	417 E 75th	★
Berry/Hill	743 Fifth Ave	73	Davis/Langdale	231 E 60th	★
Blum Helman	20 W 57th	70	Davlyn	975 Madison	39
Borgenicht	724 Fifth Ave	72	De Nagy, Tibor	41 W 57th	63
Brewster	41 W 57th	63	De Rempich	16 E 79th	13
Byron	25 E 83rd	1	Del Re, Marisa	41 E 57th	81

★ off map

ART GALLERIES UPTOWN — ALPHABETICAL (Continued)

Gallery	Address	Map No	Gallery	Address	Map No
Deutsch, Sid	20 W 57th	70	Matisse, P	41 E 57th	81
Dintenfass, T	50 W 57th	66	Mazoh, Stephen	13 E 76th	30
Donson	24 W 57th	69	McKee, David	41 E 57th	81
Dorsky	58 W 58th	62	Midtown	11 E 57th	75
Drake, Douglas	50 W 57th	66	Miller, Robt	41 E 57th	81
Drey, Paul	11 E 57th	75	Multiples	24 W 57th	69
Dyansen	11 E 57th	75	Neil Isman	1100 Madison	4
Elkon, Robt	18 E 81st	7	Newhouse	19 E 66th	54
Emmerich, A	41 E 57th	81	Niveau	962 Madison	36
Eric	25 W 56th	85	Orrefors	58 E 57th	84
Feigen, Richard	113 E 79th	23	Pace Edition/Gal	32 E 57th	82
Findlay, David	984 Madison	31	Pearl, Marilyn	38 E 57th	83
Findlay, David Jr	41 E 57th	81	Perlow, Rich/K	980 Madison	32
Findlay, Peter	1001 Madison	24	Perls	1016 Madison	17
Fischbach	24 W 57th	69	Portnoy, Theo	360 E 55th	★
Fitch-Febvrel	5 E 57th	74	Protetch, Max	37 W 57th	64
Forum	1018 Madison	16	Raydon	1091 Madison	5
Fourcade, X	36 E 75th	40	Reece Galleries	24 W 57th	69
Frumkin, Allan	50 W 57th	66	Rolly/Michaux	943 Madison	41
Galerie Naive	145 E 92nd	★	Ronin	605 Madison	80
Galer. St Etienne	24 W 57th	69	Rosenberg, Alex	20 W 57th	70
Galer. Schreiner	1046 Madison	8	Rosenberg, Paul	20 E 79th	15
Gallery 84	30 W 57th	68	Rosenberg/Stieb	32 E 57th	82
Gimpel & W	724 Fifth Ave	72	Safani	960 Madison	37
Goodman, Jas	41 E 57th	81	Saidenberg	1018 Madison	16
Goodman, M	24 W 57th	69	Salander-O'Reilly	22 E 80th	10
Graham	1014 Madison	18	Schaeffer	983 Park Ave	2
Grand Central	24 W 57th	69	Schiller-Wapner	1 E 61st	60
Hamilton, M	19 E 71st	46	Schoelkopf, Robt	50 W 57th	66
Hammer	33 W 57th	65	Schweitzer	1015 Madison	20
Heidenberg	50 W 57th	66	Sculpture Center	167 E 69th	★
Hirschl/Adler	21 E 70th	49	Shippee	41 E 57th	63
Hirschl/Adlr Mod	851 Madison	50	Siegel, Ruth	24 W 57th	69
Hutton, L	33 E 74th	43	Sindin	1035 Madison	12
IBM Gallery	Madison at 56	79	Smith	1045 Madison	9
Isselbacher	41 E 78th	21	Solomon, Holly	724 Fifth Ave	72
Jacobson, B	50 W 57th	66	Sotheby's	1334 York Ave	★
Janis, Sidney	110 W 57th	★	Spanierman	50 E 78th	28
Johnson, Jay	1044 Madison	11	Sportsman's Edge	136 E 74th	45
Jordan/Volpe	958 Madison	38	Staempfli	47 E 77th	26
Kennedy	40 W 57th	67	Steuben	715 Fifth Ave	86
Kenneth Lux	1021 Madison	19	Sumers, Martin	50 W 57th	66
Kent Fine Arts	41 E 57th	81	Tatistcheff	50 W 57th	66
Kerr, Coe	49 E 82nd	6	Uptown	1194 Madison	★
Knoedler	19 E 70th	48	Urban Center	457 Madison	★
Kovesday, P	19 E 71st	46	Urdang, Bertha	23 E 74th	42
Kraushaar	724 Fifth Ave	72	Vercel, Felix	710 Madison	59
Krugier, Jan	41 E 57th	81	Viridian	52 W 57th	66
La Boetie	9 E 82nd	3	Wally Findlay	17 E 57th	78
La Magna, Carlo	50 W 57th	66	Ward, Michael	9 E 93rd	★
Lafayette Parke	58 E 79th	22	Washburn	41 E 57th St	81
Le Loup	1044 Madison	11	Weintraub	988 Madison	25
Lefebre	411 West End	★	Wildenstein	19 E 64th St	57
Luhring, Aug	41 E 57th	81	Wittenborn	1018 Madison	16
Madison Ave	985 Madison	33	York, Richard	21 E 65th	56
Marlborough	40 W 57th	67	Zabriskie	724 Fifth Ave	72
Mathes, Barbara	851 Madison	50	Zarre, Andre	41 E 57th	81

62

★ off map

SOHO ART GALLERIES—BY MAP NUMBER

1 Circle
2 Cooper, Paul
3 Vorpal
5 Meisel
6 Terrain
7 Littlejohn Smith
8 Pindar
9 Castelli,Leo
  Sperone, Weber
10 Kind, Phyllis
11 Thorp, Edward
12 Bess Cutler
  Amos, Atlantic
13 New Contemp Mus

14 Phoenix, Stark
15 Baskerville/Wtson
16 Ward-Nasse
17 Castelli, Sonnabend
  Charles Cowles
  49th Parallel
  Germans Van Eck
18 Davidson, Max
  Gruenebaum, Haller
  Ingber, Witkin
  Munroe, Victoria
19 Mary Boone
20 Hoffman, Nancy
21 Eclipse

22 SoHo Center
23 Gladstone, B
24 Brown, Diane
25 Milliken, Alex
26 Camp, J
27 O. K. Harris
28 Vasarely Center
29 Alexander, B
30 Gallery Henoch
31 Heller
32 Dyansen
33 Rosa Esman
34 So Ho 20
35 55 Mercer

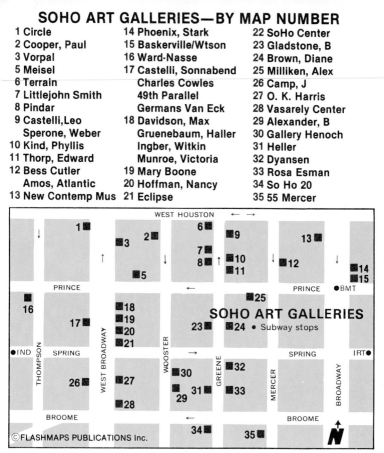

Gallery	Address	Map No
Alexander, B	59 Wooster	29
Amos Eno	164 Mercer	12
Atlantic	164 Mercer	12
Baskerville/Wtsn	578 B'way	15
Bess Cutler	164 Mercer	12
Brown, Diane	100 Greene	24
Camp, J	380 B'way	26
Castelli, Leo	420 W B'way	17
Castelli, Leo	142 Greene	9
Charles Cowles	420 W B'way	17
Circle	468 W B'way	1
Cooper, Paula	155 Wooster	2
Davidson, Max	415 B'way	18
Dyansen	122 Spring	32
Eclipse	157 Spring	21
55 Mercer	55 Mercer	35
49th Parallel	420 W B'way	17
Gallery Henoch	80 Wooster	30
Germans Van Eck	420 W B'way	17
Gladstone, B	99 Greene	23
Gruenebaum	415 B'way	18
Haller, Stephen	415 W B'way	18
Heller	71 Greene	31
Hoffman, Nancy	429 W B'way	20
Ingber	415 W B'way	18
Kind, Phyllis	136 Greene	10
Littlejohn Smith	133 Greene	7
Mary Boone	417 W B'way	19
Meisel	141 Prince	5
Milliken, Alex	98 Prine	25
Munroe, Victoria	415 B'way	18
New Contmp Mus	583 B'way	13
O. K. Harris	383 W B'way	27
Phoenix	568 B'way	14
Pindar	127 Greene	8
Rosa Esman	70 Greene	33
So Ho Center	114 Prince	22
So Ho 20	469 Broome	34
Sonnabend	420 W B'way	17
Sperone	142 Greene	9
Stark, E. L.	568 B'way	14
Terrain	141 Greene	6
Thorp, Edward	103 Prince	11
Vasarely Center	484 Broome	28
Vorpal	465 W B'way	3
Ward-Nasse	178 Prince	16
Weber, John	142 Greene	9
Witkin	415 W B'way	18

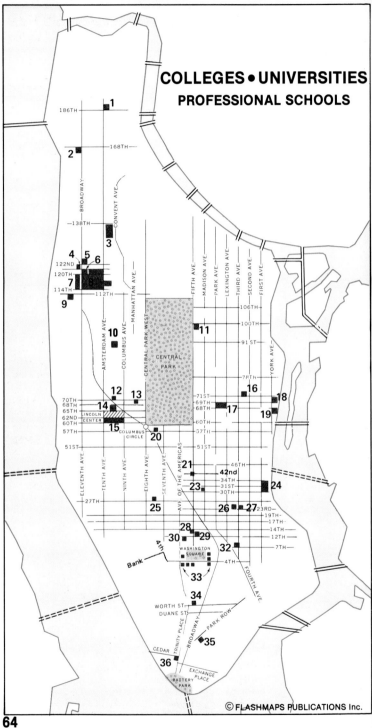

COLLEGES • UNIVERSITIES
PROFESSIONAL SCHOOLS

© FLASHMAPS PUBLICATIONS Inc.

COLLEGES & UNIVERSITIES—BY MAP NUMBERS

1 Yeshiva University	12 NY Institute of Tech	25 Fashion Institute
2 Columbia Physicians	14 Juilliard School Music	26 Baruch College
3 City College	14 School Amer Ballet	27 School Visual Arts
4 Manhattan Music	15 Fordham Ed/Law/SS	28 Parsons
5 Jewish Theological	15 John Jay	29 Yeshiva Law
6 Union Theological	16 Marymount/Manhattan	30 New School
7 Barnard College	17 Hunter College	32 Cooper Union
8 Columbia University	18 Cornell Medical	33 Hebrew Union
8 Columbia Social Work	19 Rockefeller University	33 New York Univ
8 Teachers College	20 Art Students League	33 NYU Law
9 Bank Street	21 City Univ Graduate	34 New York Law
10 Mannes School	23 Amer Academy Drama	35 Pace
11 Mt Sinai Medical	24 NYU Medical	36 NYU Business

COLLEGES & UNIVERSITIES—ALPHABETICAL

College	Address	Map No	Telephone
American Academy Dramatic Arts	120 Madison Avenue	23	686-9244
Art Students League	215 W 57th Street	20	247-4510
Bank Street College of Education	610 W 112th Street	9	663-7200
Barnard College	3009 B'way at 120th St	7	280-5262
Baruch College	55 E 24th Street	26	725-3000
Cardozo Law (Yeshiva Univ)	55 Fifth Avenue	29	790-0200
City College of New York	Convent & 138th Street	3	690-6977
City University Graduate	33 W 42nd Street	21	790-4395
Columbia Physicians/Surgeons	630 W 168th Street	2	305-3596
Columbia School Social Work	622 W 113th Street	8	280-4088
Columbia University	Broadway & 116th St	8	280-1754
Cooper Union	41 Cooper Sq at 7thSt	32	254-6300
Cornell University Medical	1300 York Avenue	18	472-5673
Fashion Institute Technology	227 W 27th Street	25	760-7675
Fordham Law	140 W 62nd Street	15	841-5189
Fordham Education/SS	Columbus Ave & 60th St	15	841-5430
Hebrew Union School Ed/Religion	1 W 4th Street	33	674-5300
Hunter College	695 Park Avenue	17	772-4000
Jewish Theological Seminary	Broadway & 122nd St	5	678-8000
John Jay College	444 W 56th Street	15	489-5183
Juilliard School of Music	Lincoln Center Plz at 66th	14	799-5000
Manhattan School of Music	120 Claremont	4	749-2802
Mannes School of Music	150 W 85th Street	10	580-0210
Marymount Manhattan	221 E 71st Street	16	535-5055
Mount Sinai School of Medicine	Fifth Ave & 100th Street	11	650-6696
New School Social Research	66 W 12th Street	30	741-5600
NY Institute of Technology	1855 Broadway	12	399-8300
New York Law	57 Worth Street	34	431-2100
New York University	Washington Square	33	998-1212
NYU Business/Public Admin.	100 Trinity Place	36	285-6000
NYU Law	40 Washington Sq South	33	998-6060
NYU Medical	550 First Avenue	24	340-5290
Pace University	1 Pace Plaza	35	488-1200
Parsons School of Design	66 Fifth Avenue	28	741-8900
Rockefeller University	York Ave & 66th Street	19	570-8000
School of American Ballet	144 W 66th Street	14	877-0600
School of Visual Arts	209 E 23rd Street	27	679-7350
Teachers College Columbia	525 W 120th Street	8	678-3000
Union Theological Seminary	Broadway & 120th St	6	662-7100
Yeshiva University	Amsterdam Ave & 185th	1	960-5400

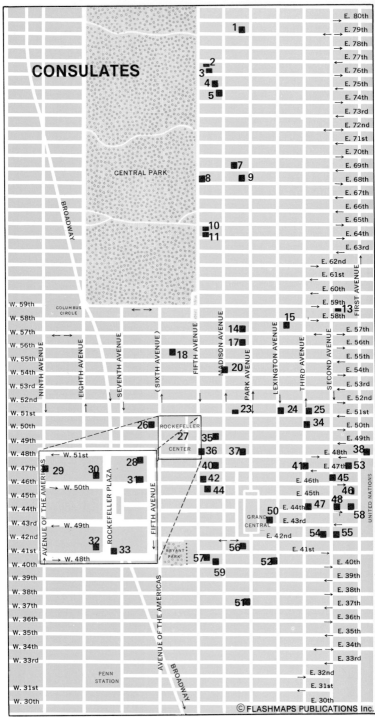

CONSULATES

CENTRAL PARK

BROADWAY

COLUMBUS CIRCLE

ROCKEFELLER CENTER

ROCKEFELLER PLAZA

AVENUE OF THE AMERICAS

FIFTH AVENUE

GRAND CENTRAL

BRYANT PARK

PENN STATION

UNITED NATIONS

FIRST AVENUE

SECOND AVENUE

THIRD AVENUE

LEXINGTON AVENUE

PARK AVENUE

MADISON AVENUE

FIFTH AVENUE

(SIXTH AVENUE)

SEVENTH AVENUE

EIGHTH AVENUE

NINTH AVENUE

W. 59th
W. 58th
W. 57th
W. 56th
W. 55th
W. 54th
W. 53rd
W. 52nd
W. 51st
W. 50th
W. 49th
W. 48th
W. 47th
W. 46th
W. 45th
W. 44th
W. 43rd
W. 42nd
W. 41st
W. 40th
W. 39th
W. 38th
W. 37th
W. 36th
W. 35th
W. 34th
W. 33rd
W. 31st
W. 30th

E. 80th
E. 79th
E. 78th
E. 77th
E. 76th
E. 75th
E. 74th
E. 73rd
E. 72nd
E. 71st
E. 70th
E. 69th
E. 68th
E. 67th
E. 66th
E. 65th
E. 64th
E. 63rd
E. 62nd
E. 61st
E. 60th
E. 59th
E. 58th
E. 57th
E. 56th
E. 55th
E. 54th
E. 53rd
E. 52nd
E. 51st
E. 50th
E. 49th
E. 48th
E. 47th
E. 46th
E. 45th
E. 44th
E. 43rd
E. 42nd
E. 41st
E. 40th
E. 39th
E. 38th
E. 37th
E. 36th
E. 35th
E. 34th
E. 33rd
E. 32nd
E. 31st
E. 30th

W. 51st
W. 50th
W. 49th
W. 48th

© FLASHMAPS PUBLICATIONS Inc.

66

CONSULATES—ALPHABETICAL

Consulate-Address	Map No.	Telephone	Consulate-Address	Map No.	Telephone
Argentina 12 W 56th	18	603-0400	**Japan** 299 Park Av	37	371-8222
Australia 636 5th Av	28	245-4000	**Kenya** 424 Madison Av	35	486-1300
Austria 31 E 69th	7	737-6400	**Kuwait** 801 2nd Av	48	687-8285
Bahamas 767 3rd Av	34	421-6420	**Korea** 460 Park Av	17	752-1700
Bangladesh 821 UN Plz	46	867-3434	**Lebanon** 9 E 76th	3	744-7905
Barbados 800 2nd Av	55	867-8435	**Liberia** 820 2nd Av	48	687-1033
Belgium 50 Rckfellr Plz	30	586-5110	**Lithuania** 41 W 82nd	★	877-4552
Bolivia 211 E 43rd	51	687-0530	**Luxembourg** 801 2nd Av	54	370-9850
Brazil 630 5th Av	31	757-3085	**Madagascar** 801 2nd Av	48	986-9491
Burma 10 E 77th	2	535-1310	**Malaysia** 140 E 45th	47	490-2722
Canada 1251 Av Amer	26	586-2400	**Malta** 249 E 35th	60	725-2345
Chile 866 Un Plz	38	980-3366	**Mexico** 8 E 41st	57	689-0456
China,P. R. 520 12th Av	★	279-0885	**Monaco** 845 3rd Av	25	759-5227
Colombia 10 E 46th	44	949-9898	**Morocco** 437 5th Av	57	758-2625
Costa Rica 80 Wall St	★	425-2620	**Nepal** 820 2nd Av	48	370-4188
Cyprus 13 E 40th	59	686-6016	**Netherlands** 1 Rckf Plz	32	246-1429
Denmark 825 Third Av	34	223-4545	**New Zealand** 630 5th Av	31	698-4650
Dominican 17 W 60th St	★	265-0630	**Nigeria** 575 Lexington	24	715-7200
Ecuador 18 E 41	59	683-7555	**Norway** 825 3rd Av	34	421-7333
Egypt 1110 2nd Av	13	759-7120	**Pakistan** 12 E 65th	10	879-5800
El Salvador 46 Park Av	51	889-3608	**Panama** 1270 6th Av	29	246-3771
Estonia 9 Rockfeller Plz	33	247-1450	**Paraguay** 1 World Trade	★	432-0733
Finland 540 Madison	20	832-6550	**Peru** 805 3rd Av	34	644-2850
France 934 5th Av	4	606-3688	**Philippines** 556 5th Av	42	764-1300
Germany 460 Park Av	15	308-8700	**Poland** 233 Madison	★	889-8360
Ghana 19 E 47th	40	832-1300	**Portugal** 630 5th Av	31	765-2980
Great Britain 845 3rd Av	25	752-8400	**San Marino** 350 5th Av	★	736-3911
Greece 69 E 79th	1	988-5500	**Saudi Arabia** 866 Un Plz	38	752-2740
Grenada 820 2nd Av	48	599-0301	**South Africa** 326 E 48th	38	371-7997
Guatemala 57 Park Ave	51	686-3837	**Spain** 150 E 58th	15	355-4080
Guyana 622 3rd Av	52	953-0920	**Sri Lanka** 630 3rd Av	52	986-7040
Haiti 60 E 42nd	56	697-9767	**St Vincent** 41 E 42nd	49	687-4490
Honduras 18 E 41st	59	889-3858	**Sudan** 210 E 49th	41	421-2680
Hungary 8 E 75th	5	879-4127	**Sweden** 825 3rd Av	34	751-5900
Iceland 370 Lexington	52	686-4100	**Switzerland** 444 Madisn	35	758-2560
India 3 E 64th	11	879-7800	**Thailand** 53 Park Pl	★	732-8166
Indonesia 5 E 68th	8	879-0600	**Trinidad Tobago** -420 Lex	50	682-7272
Ireland 515 Mad Av	20	319-2555	**Turkey** 821 UN Plz	46	949-0160
Israel 800 2nd Av	55	697-5500	**Uruguay** 747 3rd	34	753-8193
Italy 690 Park Av	9	737-9100	**Venezuela** 7 E 51st	23	826-1660
Jamaica 866 2nd Av	45	935-9000	**Yugoslavia** 767 Third Av	41	838-2300

UNITED NATIONS MISSIONS - without New York Consulates

Afghanistan	866 UN Plz	754-1191	**Mauritius**	221 E 43rd	949-0190
Bahrain	2 UN Plaza	223-6200	**Mongolia**	6 E 77th	861-9460
Botswana	866 2nd Av	759-6587	**Nicaragua**	820 2nd Av	490-7997
Burkina Faso	115 E 73rd	861-2833	**Niger**	417 E 50th	421-3260
Byelorussian	136 E 67th	535-3420	**Oman**	866 UN Plz	355-3505
Cameroon	22 E 73rd	794-2295	**P.L.O.**	115 E 65th	288-8500
Centrl Africa	386 Pk Av S	689-6195	**Qatar**	747 3rd Av	486-9335
Congo	14 E 65th	744-7840	**St Lucia**	41 E 42nd	697-9360
Cuba	315 Lex	689-7215	**St Vincent**	801 2nd Av	687-4490
Ethiopia	866 UN Plz	421-1830	**Senegal**	238 E 68th	517-9030
Gabon	820 2nd Av	867-3100	**Sierra Leone**	57 E 64th	570-0030
Gambia	19 E 47th	752-6213	**Somalia**	53 E 80th	570-9311
Germany Dem	58 Park Av	686-2596	**Surinam**	1 UN Plz	826-0660
Guinea	820 2nd Av	486-9170	**Syrian Arab**	820 2nd Av	661-1313
Guinea-Bissau	211 E 43rd	661-3977	**Tanzania**	205 E 42nd	972-9160
Iran	622 3rd Av	687-2020	**Tunisia**	405 Lex Av	557-3344
Iraq	14 E 79th	737-4433	**Ukraine**	136 E 67th	535-3418
Ivory Coast	46 E 74th	988-3930	**Un.Arab Emir.**	747 3rd Av	371-0480
Jordan	866 UN Plz	752-0135	**U.S.A.**	799 UN Plz	415-4000
Laos	321 E 45th	986-0227	**U.S.S.R.**	136 E 67th	861-4900
Lesotho	866 UN Plz	421-7543	**Yemen**	747 3rd Av	355-1730
Mauritania	9 E 77th	737-7780	**Zambia**	237 E 52nd	758-1110

★ off map

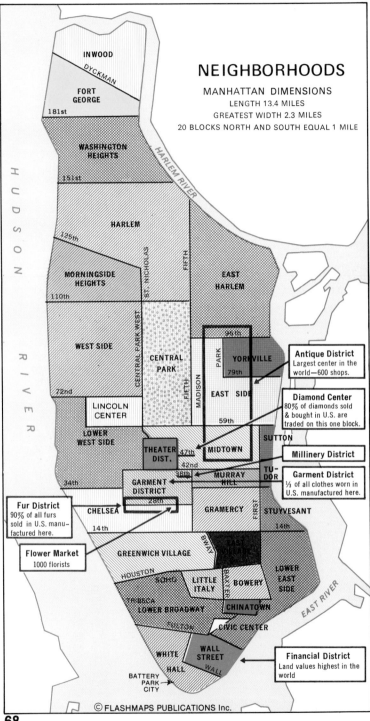

NEIGHBORHOODS

MANHATTAN DIMENSIONS
LENGTH 13.4 MILES
GREATEST WIDTH 2.3 MILES
20 BLOCKS NORTH AND SOUTH EQUAL 1 MILE

INWOOD

DYCKMAN

FORT GEORGE

181st

WASHINGTON HEIGHTS

151st

HARLEM

125th

MORNINGSIDE HEIGHTS

110th

ST. NICHOLAS

FIFTH

EAST HARLEM

HUDSON RIVER

HARLEM RIVER

CENTRAL PARK WEST

WEST SIDE

72nd

CENTRAL PARK

FIFTH

MADISON

PARK

96th

YORKVILLE

79th

EAST SIDE

59th

Antique District
Largest center in the world—600 shops.

LINCOLN CENTER

LOWER WEST SIDE

THEATER DIST.

47th

MIDTOWN

SUTTON

Diamond Center
80% of diamonds sold & bought in U.S. are traded on this one block.

42nd

38th

MURRAY HILL

TU-DOR

Millinery District

34th

GARMENT DISTRICT

28th

CHELSEA

14th

GRAMERCY

FIRST

STUYVESANT

14th

Garment District
⅓ of all clothes worn in U.S. manufactured here.

Fur District
90% of all furs sold in U.S. manu-factured here.

Flower Market
1000 florists

GREENWICH VILLAGE

BWAY

EAST

HOUSTON

SOHO

BAXTER

LITTLE ITALY

BOWERY

LOWER EAST SIDE

TRIBECA

LOWER BROADWAY

CHINATOWN

FULTON

CIVIC CENTER

EAST RIVER

WHITE

HALL

WALL STREET

WALL

BATTERY PARK CITY

Financial District
Land values highest in the world

© FLASHMAPS PUBLICATIONS Inc.

68

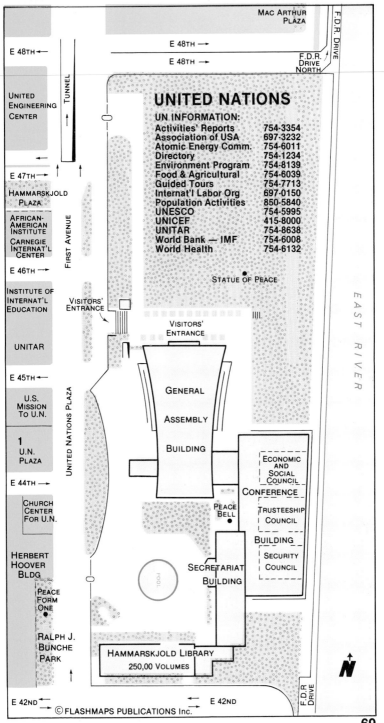

MAC ARTHUR PLAZA

F.D.R. DRIVE

E 48TH ←

E 48TH →

E 48TH →

F.D.R. DRIVE NORTH

UNITED ENGINEERING CENTER

TUNNEL

E 47TH →

HAMMARSKJOLD PLAZA

AFRICAN-AMERICAN INSTITUTE

CARNEGIE INTERNAT'L CENTER

E 46TH →

INSTITUTE OF INTERNAT'L EDUCATION

UNITAR

E 45TH ←

U.S. MISSION TO U.N.

1 U.N. PLAZA

E 44TH →

CHURCH CENTER FOR U.N.

HERBERT HOOVER BLDG

PEACE FORM ONE

RALPH J. BUNCHE PARK

E 42ND

FIRST AVENUE

UNITED NATIONS PLAZA

VISITORS' ENTRANCE

UNITED NATIONS

UN INFORMATION:

Activities' Reports	754-3354
Association of USA	697-3232
Atomic Energy Comm.	754-6011
Directory	754-1234
Environment Program	754-8139
Food & Agricultural	754-6039
Guided Tours	754-7713
Internat'l Labor Org	697-0150
Population Activities	850-5840
UNESCO	754-5995
UNICEF	415-8000
UNITAR	754-8638
World Bank — IMF	754-6008
World Health	754-6132

STATUE OF PEACE

VISITORS' ENTRANCE

GENERAL ASSEMBLY BUILDING

PEACE BELL

ECONOMIC AND SOCIAL COUNCIL

CONFERENCE

TRUSTEESHIP COUNCIL

BUILDING

SECURITY COUNCIL

SECRETARIAT BUILDING

POOL

EAST RIVER

HAMMARSKJOLD LIBRARY
250,00 VOLUMES

N

E 42ND

F.D.R DRIVE

© FLASHMAPS PUBLICATIONS INC.

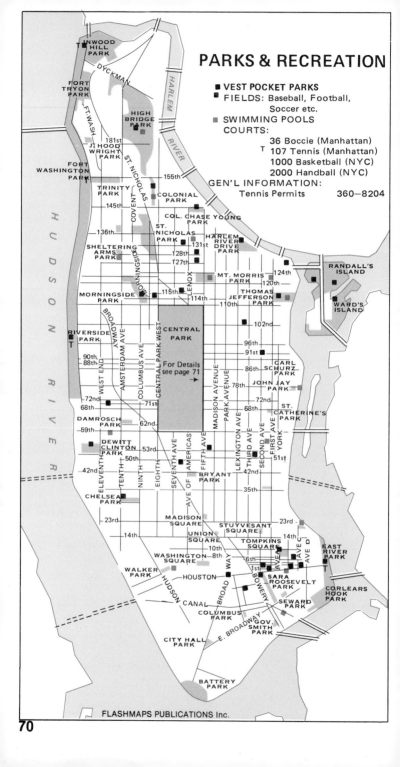

PARKS & RECREATION

- ■ VEST POCKET PARKS
- ■ FIELDS: Baseball, Football, Soccer etc.
- ■ SWIMMING POOLS

COURTS:
- 36 Boccie (Manhattan)
- T 107 Tennis (Manhattan)
- 1000 Basketball (NYC)
- 2000 Handball (NYC)

GEN'L INFORMATION:
Tennis Permits   360—8204

INWOOD HILL PARK
DYCKMAN
FORT TRYON PARK
FT. WASH.
HIGH BRIDGE PARK
J. HOOD WRIGHT PARK
181st
FORT WASHINGTON PARK
ST. NICHOLAS
155th
TRINITY PARK
COLONIAL PARK
145th
COL. CHASE YOUNG PARK
COVENT
136th
ST. NICHOLAS PARK
HARLEM RIVER DRIVE PARK
SHELTERING ARMS PARK
131st
128th
127th
124th
RANDALL'S ISLAND
MORNINGSIDE
MT. MORRIS PARK
120th
LENOX
115th
114th
WARD'S ISLAND
MORNINGSIDE PARK
THOMAS JEFFERSON PARK
110th
102nd
BROADWAY
CENTRAL PARK WEST
CENTRAL PARK
96th
91st
CARL SCHURZ PARK
90th
88th
RIVERSIDE PARK
For Details see page 71 →
86th
78th
JOHN JAY PARK
MADISON AVENUE
PARK AVENUE
WEST END
AMSTERDAM AVE
COLUMBUS AVE
72nd
72nd
68th
ST. CATHERINE'S
71st
68th
DAMROSCH PARK
62nd
59th
LEXINGTON AVE
THIRD AVE
SECOND AVE
FIRST AVE
YORK
51st
DEWITT CLINTON PARK
53rd
50th
ELEVENTH
TENTH
NINTH
EIGHTH
SEVENTH AVE
AVE OF AMERICAS
FIFTH AVE
42nd
42nd
BRYANT PARK
35th
CHELSEA PARK
23rd
23rd
MADISON SQUARE
STUYVESANT SQUARE
14th
UNION SQUARE
14th
TOMPKINS SQUARE
AVE C
AVE D
WASHINGTON SQUARE
10th
8th
6th
EAST RIVER PARK
WALKER PARK
BROADWAY
1st
BOWERY
SARA ROOSEVELT PARK
HUDSON
HOUSTON
CANAL
SEWARD PARK
CORLEARS HOOK PARK
COLUMBUS PARK
E. BROADWAY
GOV. SMITH PARK
CITY HALL PARK
BATTERY PARK

HARLEM RIVER

HUDSON RIVER

FLASHMAPS PUBLICATIONS Inc.

70

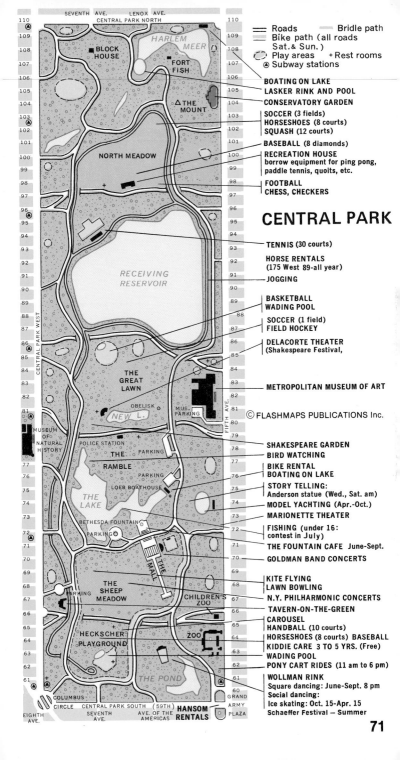

CENTRAL PARK

Roads ═══   **Bridle path**

Bike path (all roads Sat. & Sun.)

⌐ **Play areas**   **+ Rest rooms**

ⓐ **Subway stations**

SEVENTH AVE.   LENOX AVE.
CENTRAL PARK NORTH

HARLEM MEER

BLOCK HOUSE

FORT FISH

△ THE MOUNT

NORTH MEADOW

RECEIVING RESERVOIR

CENTRAL PARK WEST

THE GREAT LAWN

OBELISK

NEW L.

MUS. PARKING

FIFTH AVE.

MUSEUM OF NATURAL HISTORY

POLICE STATION

PARKING

THE RAMBLE

PARKING

LOEB BOATHOUSE

THE LAKE

BETHESDA FOUNTAIN

PARKING

THE MALL

PARKING

THE SHEEP MEADOW

CHILDREN'S ZOO

HECKSCHER PLAYGROUND

ZOO

THE POND

COLUMBUS CIRCLE

CENTRAL PARK SOUTH (59TH)

SEVENTH AVE.

AVE. OF THE AMERICAS

EIGHTH AVE.

GRAND ARMY PLAZA

HANSOM RENTALS

BOATING ON LAKE
LASKER RINK AND POOL
CONSERVATORY GARDEN
SOCCER (3 fields)
HORSESHOES (8 courts)
SQUASH (12 courts)
BASEBALL (8 diamonds)
RECREATION HOUSE
borrow equipment for ping pong, paddle tennis, quoits, etc.
FOOTBALL
CHESS, CHECKERS

TENNIS (30 courts)

HORSE RENTALS
(175 West 89-all year)
JOGGING

BASKETBALL
WADING POOL

SOCCER (1 field)
FIELD HOCKEY

DELACORTE THEATER
(Shakespeare Festival,

METROPOLITAN MUSEUM OF ART

© FLASHMAPS PUBLICATIONS Inc.

SHAKESPEARE GARDEN
BIRD WATCHING
BIKE RENTAL
BOATING ON LAKE
STORY TELLING:
Anderson statue (Wed., Sat. am)
MODEL YACHTING (Apr.-Oct.)
MARIONETTE THEATER
FISHING (under 16:
contest in July)
THE FOUNTAIN CAFE June-Sept.
GOLDMAN BAND CONCERTS

KITE FLYING
LAWN BOWLING
N.Y. PHILHARMONIC CONCERTS
TAVERN-ON-THE-GREEN
CAROUSEL
HANDBALL (10 courts)
HORSESHOES (8 courts) BASEBALL
KIDDIE CARE 3 TO 5 YRS. (Free)
WADING POOL
PONY CART RIDES (11 am to 6 pm)
WOLLMAN RINK
Square dancing: June-Sept. 8 pm
Social dancing:
Ice skating: Oct. 15-Apr. 15
Schaeffer Festival — Summer

71

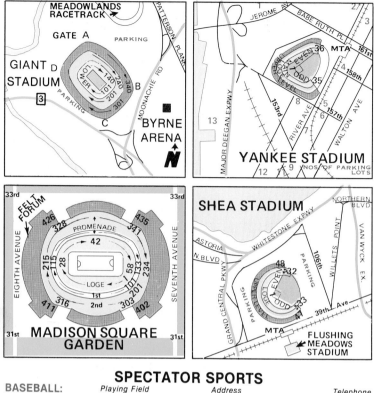

SPECTATOR SPORTS

	Playing Field	Address	Telephone
BASEBALL:			
NY Mets	**Shea Stadium**	Flushing, NY	(718) 507-8499
NY Yankees	**Yankee Stadium**	Bronx, NY	(212) 293-6000
BASKETBALL:			
NY Knicks	**Madison Sq Garden**	Seventh Ave & 32nd	(212) 563-8000
NJ Nets	**Brendan Byrne Arena**	Meadowlands, NJ	(201) 935-3900
FOOTBALL:			
NY Giants	**Giant Stadium**	Meadowlands, NJ	(201) 935-8222
NY Jets	**Giant Stadium**	Meadowlands, NJ	(212) 935-8222
HOCKEY:			
NJ Devils	**Brendan Byrne Arena**	Meadowlands, NJ	(201) 935-6050
NY Islanders	**Nassau Coliseum**	Uniondale, LI	(516) 794-4100
NY Rangers	**Madison Sq Garden**	Seventh Ave & 32nd	(212) 563-8000
HORSE RACING:			
Aqueduct Race Track		Rockaway Blvd, Ozone Park	(718) 641-4700
Belmont Raceway		Hempstead Tpke, Belmont, LI	(718) 641-4700
Meadowlands Race Track		Meadowlands, New Jersey	(201) 460-4079
Roosevelt Raceway		Westbury, Long Island	(516) 222-2000
Yonkers Raceway		Yonkers Ave, Yonkers, NY	(914) 968-4200

ANNUAL SPORTING EVENTS

Colgate Grand Prix Tennis (Jan)
Golden Gloves Boxing (Jan-Feb)
International Horse Show (Nov)

MADISON SQUARE GARDEN 563-8300

Millrose Wanamaker Track (Jan-Feb)
Nat'l Invitation Tournament (Mar)
Westminster Kennel Show (Feb)

NY Marathon - 26½ miles thru 5 boroughs - last Sun of Oct (212) 860-4455
US Open Tennis - Flushing Meadows, N.Y. (Sept) (718) 271-5100
Sports Complex Info - Meadowlands, N. J. (201) 935-3900

72

SKYSCRAPERS AND BEST VIEWS

★ Best panoramic views

MIDTOWN MANHATTAN

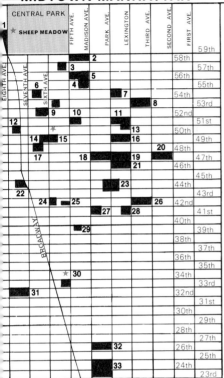

LOWER MANHATTAN

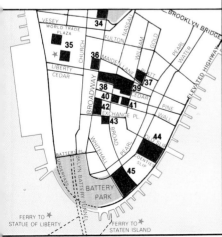

SKYSCRAPERS

Building · No. stories	Height in ft.	Map No.
World Trade · 110	1,350	35
Empire State · 102	1,250	30
Chrysler · 77	1,046	26
American Interntl · 66	950	41
40 Wall Tower · 71	927	40
Citicorp Center · 54	914	8
RCA Rockefeller · 70	850	15
Chase Manhattan · 60	813	39
Pan Am · 59	808	23
Woolworth · 58	792	34
1 Penn Plaza · 57	764	31
1 Liberty Place · 52	743	36
Citibank · 56	741	7
20 Exchange Pl · 47	741	43
Exxon · 54	735	14
1 Astor Place · 54	730	22
9 W 57th · 52	725	3
Union Carbide · 52	707	18
General Motors · 50	705	2
Metropolitan Life · 50	700	33
500 Fifth · 60	697	25
Chem-NY Trust · 50	687	19
55 Water · 53	686	44
Chanin · 56	680	28
Gulf & Western · 44	679	1
Marine Midland · 52	677	38
McGraw Hill · 51	674	17
Lincoln · 54	673	27
1633 Broadway · 48	670	12
Trump Tower · 68	664	5
Museum Towers · 54	650	9
American Brands · 47	648	21
AT & T · 37	647	4
Irving Trust · 52	640	42
345 Park Ave · 44	634	11
Grace · 50	636	24
1 N.Y. Plaza · 50	630	45
Home Insurance · 44	630	37
1 Hammarskjold · 50	628	20
Burlington House · 50	625	6
Waldorf Astoria · 47	625	16
Olympic Towers · 51	620	10
10 E 40th · 48	620	29
General Electric · 51	616	13
N.Y. Life · 36	615	32
J.C. Penney · 46	609	9
I.B.M. · 41	607	5

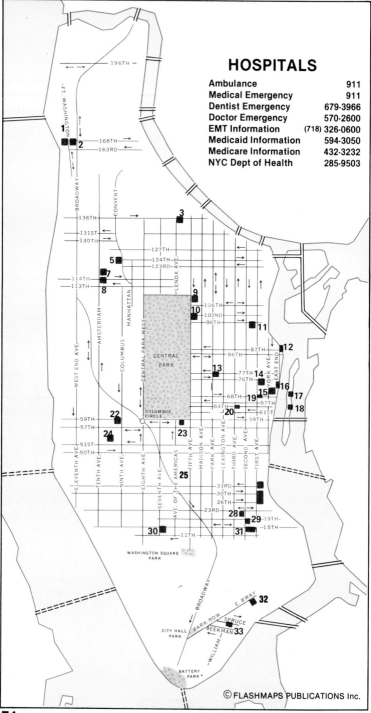

HOSPITALS

Ambulance	911
Medical Emergency	911
Dentist Emergency	679-3966
Doctor Emergency	570-2600
EMT Information	(718) 326-0600
Medicaid Information	594-3050
Medicare Information	432-3232
NYC Dept of Health	285-9503

© FLASHMAPS PUBLICATIONS Inc.

HOSPITALS—BY MAP NUMBERS

1	Columbia Presbyterian	17	Coler Memorial
2	Babies Hospital	18	Goldwater Memorial
2	Harkness Eye Institute	19	Memorial - Sloan-Kettering
2	New York Orthopedic	20	Manhattan Eye & Ear
2	Sloane Hospital for Women	22	Roosevelt-St. Luke's
3	Harlem Hospital	23	Medical Arts
5	Sydenham Family Care	24	St. Clare's
7	Women's - Roosevelt	25	Strang Clinic
8	St. Luke's - Roosevelt	26	New York University
9	Cardinal Cooke Health Center	27	Bellevue/VA Hospitals
10	Mount Sinai	28	Cabrini-Columbus
11	Metropolitan Hospital	29	Beth Israel
12	Doctors Hospital	29	Hospital Joint Diseases
13	Lenox Hill	30	St. Vincent's
14	Gracie Square	31	New York Eye & Ear
15	New York Hospital-Cornell	32	Gouverneurs
15	Payne Whitney Pavilion	33	Beekman Downtown
16	Hospital Special Surgery	33	New York Infirmary

HOSPITALS—ALPHABETICAL

Hospital	Address	Map No	Telephone
Babies Hospital	Broadway & 166th Street	2	305-2500
Beekman Downtown	170 William Street	33	312-5000
Bellevue Medical Center	First Ave & 27th Street	27	561-4141
Beth Israel	First Ave & 16th Street	29	420-2000
Cabrini-Columbus	227 E 19th Street	28	995-6000
Cardinal Cooke Health Center	Fifth Ave & 106th Street	9	360-1000
Coler Memorial	Roosevelt Island	17	688-9400
Columbia-Presbyterian Med Ctr	Broadway & 168th Street	1	305-2500
Harkness Eye Institute	635 W 165th Street	2	305-2500
New York Orthopedic	622 W 168th Street	2	305-2500
Doctors Hospital	East End Ave & 87th	12	870-9000
Goldwater Memorial	Roosevelt Island	18	750-6800
Gouverneurs Hospital	227 Madison Street	32	374-4000
Gracie Square	420 E 76th Street	14	988-4400
Harlem Hospital	Lenox Ave & 135th Street	3	491-1234
Hospital for Joint Diseases	301 E 17th Street	29	598-6000
Hospital for Special Surgery	535 E 70th Street	16	606-1000
Lenox Hill Hospital	Park Ave & 77th Street	13	439-2345
Manhattan Eye & Ear	210 E 64th Street	20	838-9200
Medical Arts Center	57 W 57th Street	23	755-0200
Memorial - Sloan - Kettering	York Ave & 68th Street	19	794-7722
Metropolitan Hospital	First Ave & 98th Street	11	230-6262
Mount Sinai	Fifth Ave & 100th Street	10	241-6500
New York Hospital-Cornell	525 E 68th Street	15	472-5454
New York Eye & Ear	310 E 14th Street	31	598-1313
New York Infirmary	170 William Street	33	312-5000
New York University Medical Ctr	550 First Ave	26	340-7300
Payne Whitney Pavilion	525 E 68th Street	15	472-6282
Roosevelt-St. Luke's	Ninth Ave & 59th Street	22	554-7000
St. Clare's	426 W 52nd Street	24	586-1500
St. Luke's - Roosevelt Hospital	Amsterdam & 114th Street	8	870-6000
St. Vincent's	Seventh Ave & 11th Street	30	790-7000
Sloane Hospital for Women	Broadway & 166th Street	2	305-2500
Strang Clinic	55 E 34th Street	25	684-6969
Sydenham Family Care	215 W 125th St	5	678-5356
Veterans Administration	First Ave & 24th Street	27	686-7500
Women's - Roosevelt Hospital	Amsterdam Ave & 114th St	7	870-6000

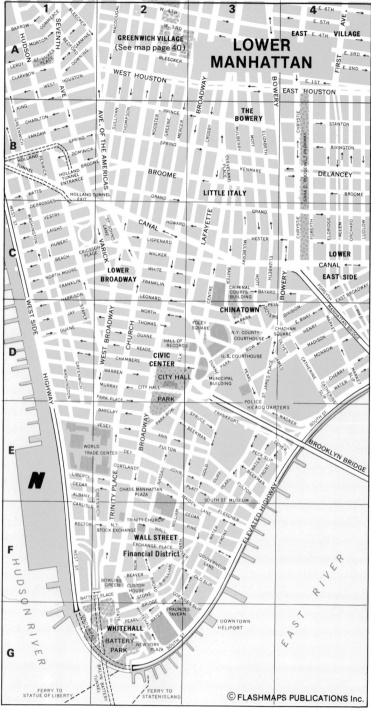

LOWER MANHATTAN STREETS—ALPHABETICAL

Street	Map Location	Street	Map Location	Street	Map Location
Albany	E-1	Elk	D-2	New	F-2
Allen	C-4	Elizabeth	B-3, C-3	Old Ship	F-3
Ann	E-2	Ericsson Pl	C-1	Oliver	D-4
Ave of Americas	B-2	Exchange Pl	F-2	Orchard	C-4
Barclay	E-2	Fletcher	F-3	Park	D-3
Barrow	A-1	Foley Square	D-3	Park Place	D-2
Battery Pl	F-1	Forsyth	C-4	Park Row	D-3, E-2
Baxter	C-3	Fourth West	A-2	Pearl	D, E-3, G-2
Bayard	C-3	Frankfort	E-3	Peck Slip	E-3
Beach	C-1	Franklin	C-1, 2	Pell	D-3
Beaver	F-2	Front	E, F-3	Pine	F-3
Bedford	A-1	Fulton	E-2, 3	Platt	E-3
Beekman	E-3	Gold	E-3	Reade	D-2
Bleecker	A-1, 2, 3	Gouverneur Lane	F-3	Rector	F-1
Bowery	A-3, C-4	Grand	B-2, C-3, 4	Rivington	B-4
Bowling Green	F-2	Greene	B-2	Roosevelt Pkwy	B-4
Bridge	F-2	Greenwich	B-1, F-2	St Johns	C-2
Broadway	A-3, E-2	Harrison	C-1	St James Pl	D-3
Broadway E	C, D-4	Henry	D-4	Second Ave	B-4
Broadway W	D-2	Hester	C-3	Seventh Ave	A-1
Broome	B-1, 2, 4	Holland Tunnel	B-1	South	G-2
Canal	C-2, 3, 4	Houston East	A-4	Spring	B-1, 2
Catherine	D-4	Houston West	A-1, 2	Spruce	E-3
Catherine Slip	D-4	Howard	C-2	Stanton	B-4
Cedar	E-1, F-3	Hubert	C-1	Staple	D-1
Centre	C-3	Hudson	A-1	State	G-2
Chambers	D-2	James	D-4	Stone	F-2
Charlton	B-1	Jay	D-1	Sullivan	B-2
Chatham Sq	D-4	Kenmare	B-3	Third West	A-2
Cherry	D-4	King	B-1	Thomas	D-2
Chrystie	C-4	Lafayette	C-3	Thompson	B-2
Church	D-2	Laight	C-1	Vandam	B-1
Civic Center	D-2	Leonard	C-2	Varick	C-2
Clarkson	A-1	Leroy	A-1	Vesey	E-2
Cleveland Pl	B-3	Liberty	E-1	Vestry	C-1
Cliff	E-3	Lispenard	C-2	Walker	C-2
Coenties Slip	F-2	Ludlow	C-4	Wall	F-2
Commerce	A-1	Macdougal	A-2	Walter	E-3
Cortlandt	E-2	Madison	D-4	Warren	D-2
Crosby	B-3	Maiden Lane	E-3	Washington	D-1
Desbrosses	C-1	Market	D-4	Water	D-4, G-2
Delancey	B-4	Market Slip	D-4	Watts	B-3
Dey	E-2	Mercer	B-2	West	C, F-1
Division	D-4	Moore North	C-1	White	C-2
Dominick	B-1	Morrow	D-4	Whitehall	G-2
Dover	E-3	Morton	A-1	William	F-2
Downing	A-1	Mott	B, C-3	William S	F-2
Doyers	D-3	Mulberry	B, C-3	Wooster	B-2
Duane	D-1, 2, 3	Murray	D-2	World Trade	E-1, 2
Eldridge	C-4	Nassau	E-2	Worth	D-2

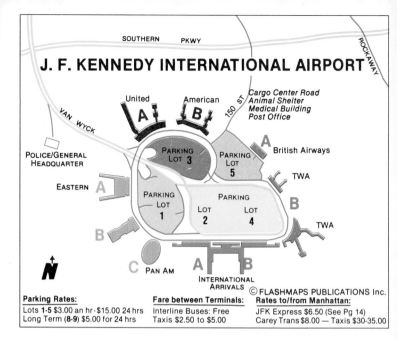

Parking Rates:
Lots **1-5** $3.00 an hr - $15.00 24 hrs
Long Term (**8-9**) $5.00 for 24 hrs

Fare between Terminals:
Interline Buses: Free
Taxis $2.50 to $5.00

Rates to/from Manhattan:
JFK Express $6.50 (See Pg 14)
Carey Trans $8.00 — Taxis $30-35.00

AIRLINES

Airline	Map Area	Telephone	Airline	Map Area	Telephone
Aer Lingus	■ B	557-1110	**Icelandair**	■ B	967-8888
Aero Argentinas	■ B	★ 327-0276	**Japan**	■ B	838-4400
Aero Mexico	■ B	391-2900	**KLM**	■ B	759-3600
Aeroflot	■ C	397-1660	**Korean**	■ B	371-4820
Air Afrique	■ A	247-0100	**Kuwait**	■ B	308-5454
Air France	■ A	247-0100	**Lan Chile**	■ B	★ 225-5526
Air India	■ A	751-6200	**Lot Polish**	■ C	869-1074
Air Jamaica	■■ A	★ 523-5585	**LTU**	■■ A	★ 421-5842
Alitalia	■ A	582-8900	**Lufthansa**	■ B	☆ 895-1277
Allegheny	■■ A	★ 428-4253	**NY Helicopter**	■ B	★ 645-3494
ALM-Antillean	■ B	★ 327-7230	**Nigeria**	■ A	935-2700
American	■■ B	431-1132	**Northwest**	■ B	★ 225-2525
American Eagle	■■ B	431-1132	**Olympic**	■■ A	838-3600
Avianca	■ C	246-5241	**Pakistan**	■ A	370-9158
British Airways	■■ A	★ 247-9297	**Pan Am**	■ C	687-2600
British Caledonia	■ A	★ 231-0270	**Piedmont**	■■ B	★ 251-5720
BWIA	■■ A	581-3200	**Royal Air Maroc**	■ B	974-1077
CAAC	■ C	656-4722	**Royal Jordan**	■ A	949-0050
China Air	■ B	399-7877	**Sabena**	■■ B	936-7800
Continental	■ A	319-9494	**SAS**	■ A	☆ 657-7700
Czechoslovak	■ C	682-5833	**Saudi Arabian**	■ C	758-4727
Delta	■ B	★ 221-1212	**Swissair**	■ A	☆ 995-8400
Dominicana	■ A	★ 635-3560	**TAP Air Portugal**	■■ A	944-2100
Eastern	■ A	986-5000	**TWA**	■ B	290-2121
Ecuatoriana	■■ B	★ 327-1348	**Tarom**	■ C	687-6013
Egyptair	■ B	581-5600	**United**	■■ A	☆ 803-2200
El Al	■ A	486-2600	**US Air**	■■ A	736-3200
Finnair	■■ A	889-7070	**Varig**	■ B	682-3100
Guyana	■ B	657-7474	**Viasa**	■ A	★ 327-5454
Iberia	■ B	☆ 793-3300	**Yugoslav**	■ C	246-6401

★ (800)- ☆ (718)   ★ (800)- ☆ (718)

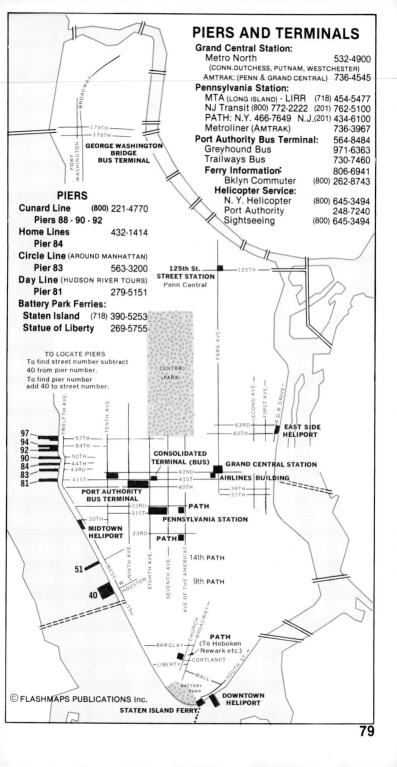

PIERS AND TERMINALS

Grand Central Station:
Metro North   532-4900
(CONN. DUTCHESS, PUTNAM, WESTCHESTER)
AMTRAK: (PENN & GRAND CENTRAL) 736-4545

Pennsylvania Station:
MTA (LONG ISLAND) - LIRR (718) 454-5477
NJ Transit (800) 772-2222 (201) 762-5100
PATH: N.Y. 466-7649 N.J.(201) 434-6100
Metroliner (AMTRAK)   736-3967

Port Authority Bus Terminal: 564-8484
Greyhound Bus   971-6363
Trailways Bus   730-7460

Ferry Information: 806-6941
Bklyn Commuter (800) 262-8743

Helicopter Service:
N. Y. Helicopter (800) 645-3494
Port Authority   248-7240
Sightseeing   (800) 645-3494

PIERS

Cunard Line   (800) 221-4770
  Piers 88 · 90 · 92

Home Lines   432-1414
  Pier 84

Circle Line (AROUND MANHATTAN)
  Pier 83   563-3200

Day Line (HUDSON RIVER TOURS)
  Pier 81   279-5151

Battery Park Ferries:
  Staten Island (718) 390-5253
  Statue of Liberty 269-5755

TO LOCATE PIERS
To find street number subtract
40 from pier number.
To find pier number
add 40 to street number.

GEORGE WASHINGTON
BRIDGE
BUS TERMINAL

BROADWAY
179TH
178TH
FORT WASHINGTON

125th St.
STREET STATION
Penn Central
125TH

CENTRAL
PARK

PARK AVE.

SECOND AVE.
FIRST AVE.
F.D.R. DRIVE

63RD
60TH
EAST SIDE
HELIPORT

TWELFTH AVE.
TENTH AVE.

97
94
92
90
84
83
81

57TH
54TH
50TH
44TH
43RD
41ST

CONSOLIDATED
TERMINAL (BUS)

42ND
41ST
40TH

GRAND CENTRAL STATION

AIRLINES BUILDING

38TH
37TH

PORT AUTHORITY
BUS TERMINAL

33RD
31ST

PATH

PENNSYLVANIA STATION

30TH

MIDTOWN
HELIPORT

23RD

PATH

WEST ST.
NINTH AVE.
EIGHTH AVE.
SEVENTH AVE.
AVE. OF THE AMERICAS

14TH PATH

9TH PATH

51

40

W. HOUSTON ST.

CHURCH
BROADWAY

PATH
(To Hoboken
Newark etc.)

BARCLAY
CORTLANDT
LIBERTY
WALL
SOUTH ST.

BATTERY
PARK

DOWNTOWN
HELIPORT

© FLASHMAPS PUBLICATIONS Inc.

STATEN ISLAND FERRY

79

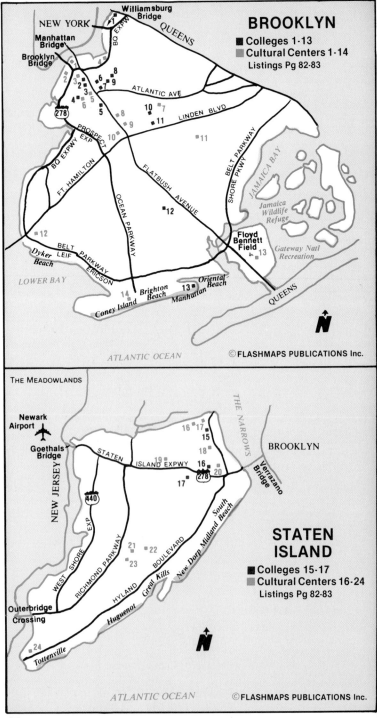

BROOKLYN

■ Colleges 1-13
▢ Cultural Centers 1-14

Listings Pg 82-83

NEW YORK
Williamsburg Bridge
Manhattan Bridge
Brooklyn Bridge
QUEENS
BQ EXPWY
ATLANTIC AVE
LINDEN BLVD
278
PROSPECT EXP
BQ EXPWY
FT HAMILTON
OCEAN PARKWAY
FLATBUSH AVENUE
BELT PARKWAY
SHORE PKWY
JAMAICA BAY
Jamaica Wildlife Refuge
Floyd Bennett Field
Gateway Natl Recreation
BELT PARKWAY
LEIF ERICSON
Dyker Beach
LOWER BAY
Brighton Beach
Coney Island
Manhattan Beach
Oriental Beach
QUEENS

ATLANTIC OCEAN

©FLASHMAPS PUBLICATIONS Inc.

THE MEADOWLANDS
Newark Airport
Goethals Bridge
NEW JERSEY
440
WEST SHORE EXP
RICHMOND PARKWAY
STATEN ISLAND EXPWY
278
THE NARROWS
BROOKLYN
Verrazano Bridge
HYLAND BOULEVARD
Great Kills
Huguenot
New Dorp
South Midland Beach
Outerbridge Crossing
Tottenville

STATEN ISLAND

■ Colleges 15-17
▢ Cultural Centers 16-24

Listings Pg 82-83

ATLANTIC OCEAN

©FLASHMAPS PUBLICATIONS Inc.

80

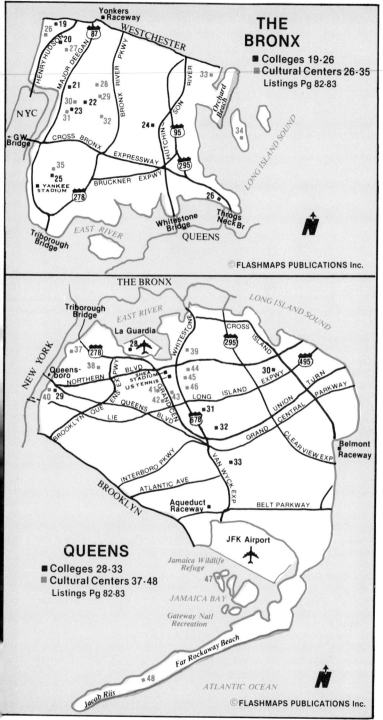

THE BRONX

■ Colleges 19-26
■ Cultural Centers 26-35
Listings Pg 82-83

Yonkers Raceway
26 ■ 19
20
27
WESTCHESTER
■ 87
HENRY HUDSON PKWY
MAJOR DEEGAN
BRONX RIVER PKWY
HUTCHINSON RIVER
33
Orchard Beach
21 ■ 28
30 ■ 29
■ 22
■ 23
31
32
24 ■
95
34
LONG ISLAND SOUND
NYC
G.W. Bridge
CROSS BRONX
EXPRESSWAY
295
35
■ 25
YANKEE STADIUM
BRUCKNER EXPWY
278
26 ■
Triborough Bridge
EAST RIVER
Whitestone Bridge
Throgs Neck Br
QUEENS

© FLASHMAPS PUBLICATIONS Inc.

THE BRONX

Triborough Bridge
EAST RIVER
LONG ISLAND SOUND
La Guardia
28
WHITESTONE
CROSS
295
ISLAND
495
NEW YORK
37
278
39
Queensboro
38
BLVD
44
30
495
NORTHERN
SHEA STADIUM
US TENNIS
45
EXPWY
TURN
QUEENS EXPWY
41
46
LONG ISLAND
UNION
PARKWAY
40
29
42
43
GRAND CEN
31
GRAND CENTRAL
LIE
678
CLEARVIEW EXP
Belmont Raceway
QUEENS
BLVD
32
BROOKLYN
INTERBORO PKWY
ATLANTIC AVE
VAN WYCK EXP
33
Aqueduct Raceway
BELT PARKWAY
BROOKLYN

JFK Airport

Jamaica Wildlife Refuge
47
JAMAICA BAY
Gateway Natl Recreation

QUEENS

■ Colleges 28-33
■ Cultural Centers 37-48
Listings Pg 82-83

Far Rockaway Beach
48
Jacob Riis
ATLANTIC OCEAN

© FLASHMAPS PUBLICATIONS Inc.

81

BRONX·BROOKLYN·QUEENS·STATEN ISLAND

CULTURAL CENTERS·HISTORIC SITES·MUSEUMS — By Map Nos

1 Empire Fulton
2 Bklyn Hgts
3 Plymouth Church
4 Bklyn Navy Yard
5 L.I. Historical
6 NY Transit
7 Bklyn Children's
8 Bklyn Museum
9 Bklyn Botanic
10 Prospect Pk Zoo
11 Wyckoff House
12 Ft. Hamilton
13 Gatwy Nat'l Rec
14 NY Aquarium
16 Snug Hrb/Gardens

17 S.I. Institute
18 S.I. Museum
19 S.I. Zoo
20 Garibaldi-Meucci
21 Marchais Tibet
22 High Rock Center
23 Richmnd/Voorlezer
24 Billopp House
26 Wave Hill
27 Van Cortlandt
28 Bronx Historic
29 NY Botanical
30 Poe Cottage
31 Hall of Fame
32 Bronx Zoo

33 Bartow-Pell
34 North Wind Mus
35 Bronx Mus of Arts
37 Noguchi Garden
38 Mus Moving Image
39 Friends' Meeting
40 Hunter's Point
41 NY Hall Science
42 Queens Zoo
43 Queens Museum
44 Bowne House
45 Queens His/Kngslnd
46 Queens Botanic
47 Jamaica Wildlife
48 Ft. Tilden

CULTURAL CENTERS·HISTORIC SITES·MUSEUMS

Name	Address	Map No	(Area 718) Telephone
Bartow-Pell Mansion-1836*	Shore Rd & Pelham Bay Pkwy, Bx	33	885-1461
Billopp Conference Hse-1680*	7445 Hyland Blvd, S.I.	24	984-2086
Bowne House-1661*	37-01 Bowne, Flushing, Q	44	359-0528
Bronx Historic-Valentine Varian	3266 Bainbridge Avenue, Bx	28	*881-8900
Bronx Museum of the Arts	1040 Grand Concourse, Bx	35	*681-6000
Bronx Zoo	Bronx Rvr Pkwy - Fordham Rd	32	*367-1010
Brooklyn Botanic Gardens	1000 Washington Ave, Bklyn	9	622-4433
Brooklyn Children's Museum	145 Brooklyn Avenue, Bklyn	7	735-4432
Brooklyn Hgts/Esplanade*	Atlantic/Fulton/Court/Montague	2	no phone
Brooklyn Museum	Eastern Pkwy/Wash Ave, Bklyn	8	638-5000
Brooklyn Navy Yard	Navy Yard, Bklyn	4	no phone
Empire Fulton Ferry Park	New Dock/Cadman Plz W, Bkln	1	858-4708
Fort Hamilton Museum	Fort Hamilton 101st St, Bklyn	12	630-4349
Fort Tilden	Ft Tilden, Breezy Point, Q	48	474-4600
Friends' Meeting Hse-1694*	137-16 Northern Blvd, Q	39	358-9636
Garibaldi-Meucci Museum	420 Tompkins Avenue, S.I.	20	442-1608
Gateway National Rec Ctrs	Hdqt Floyd Bennet Field, Bklyn	13	258-6733
High Rock Conservation Ctr*	200 Nevada Avenue, S.I.	22	987-6233
Hall of Fame Great Americans	University at W 181st St, Bx	31	*220-6312
Hunter's Point Hist Dist-1870*	45th Ave betw 21-23rd Sts Q	40	no phone
Jamaica Bay Wildlife Refuge	Broad Channel & 1st Road, Q	47	474-0613
L.I. Historical Society	128 Pierpont St Bklyn	5	624-0890
Marchais Center Tibetan Art	328 Lighthouse Avenue, S.I.	21	987-3478
Museum of Moving Image	34-31 35th St, Astoria, Q	38	630-4100
New York Aquarium	Boardwalk/W 8th, Bklyn	14	266-8711
New York Botanical Gardens*	200th St, Southern Blvd, Bx	29	*220-8777
New York Hall of Science	Flushing Meadow Park, Q	41	699-0005
New York Transit Museum	Boerum & Schermerhorn St, Bkly	6	330-3060
Noguchi Garden Museum	32-37 Vernon Blvd, L.I.C. Q	37	204-7088
North Wind Undersea Mus	610 City Island Avenue, Bx	34	*885-0701
Plymouth Church Pilgrim-1849*	Orange & Hick Street, Bklyn	3	624-4743
Poe Cottage-1812	Grand Cncrse/Kingsbrdg, Bx	30	*881-8900
Prospect Pk Zoo/Lefferts Hs	Prospect Park, Bklyn	10	965-6560
Queens Botanical Gardens	43-50 Main, Flushing, Q	46	886-3800
Queens Hist Soc Kingslnd-1774*	143-35 37th Av, Flushing Q	45	939-0647
Queens Museum	Flushing Meadow Park, Q	43	592-5555
Queens Zoo Children's Farm	Flushing Meadow Park, Q	42	699-7239

*National Historic Landmark   *(Area 212)

BRONX·BROOKLYN·QUEENS·STATEN ISLAND

CULTURAL CENTERS Continued

Richmondtown Restoration	411 Clarke Avenue, S.I.	23	351-1611
Snug Harbor Center/Gardens	Kissel Ave, Snug Hrbr Rd, S.I.	16	448-2500
S.I. Children's Museum	15 Beach Street, S.I.	18	273-2060
S.I. Institute Arts & Sciences	75 Stuyvesant Place, S.I.	17	727-1135
S.I. Zoo	614 Broadway, S.I.	19	442-3100
Van Cortlandt Mansion-1748*	B'way at W 246th St, Bx	27	*543-3344
Voorlezer's House-1695*	Arthur Kill & Center, S.I.	23	351-1611
Wave Hill-c 1844*	675 W 252nd Street, Bx	26	*549-2055
Wyckoff Pieter Claesen Hs-1652*	5816 Clarendon Road, Bklyn	11	629-5400

COLLEGES & UNIVERSITIES — By Map Numbers

1 Boricua	8 Pratt Inst	17 College S.I.	26 NY Maritime
2 Polytech Inst	9 St. Joseph's	19 Coll Mt St Vinc	28 Acad Aeronau
2 NY Tech	10 Medgar Evers	20 Manhattan	29 La Guardia
3 St. Francis	11 Downstate	21 Herb Lehman	30 Queensboro
4 Bklyn Law	12 Bklyn College	22 Fordham Univ	31 Law School
5 Bklyn Conserv	13 Kingsborough	23 Bx Communty	31 Queens Collg
6 Long Island U	15 College S.I.	24 Einstein Med	32 St. John's U
7 Bklyn Acad	16 Wagner	25 Hostos Comm	33 York College

COLLEGES & UNIVERSITIES — Alphabetical

College	Address	Map No	(Area 718) Telephone
Academy of Aeronautics	LaGuardia Airport, Q	28	429-6600
Boricua College	186 N 6th Street, Bklyn	1	782-2200
Brooklyn Academy of Music	30 Lafayette Ave, Bklyn	7	636-4100
Brooklyn College CUNY	Bedford Av & Av H, Bklyn	12	780-5485
Brooklyn Conservatory Music	58 7th Ave/Lincoln Pl, Bklyn	5	622-3300
Brooklyn Law School	342 Fulton Street, Bklyn	4	625-2200
CUNY Community Colleges			
Bronx Community	University Av & 181st St, Bx	23	*220-6450
Hostos Community	475 Grand Concourse, Bx	25	*960-1200
Kingsborough Community	2001 Oriental Blvd, Bklyn	13	934-5000
La Guardia Community	31-10 Thomson Street, Q	29	482-5000
Medgar Evers Community	1150 Carroll Street, Bklyn	10	735-1750
NYC Applied Arts	300 Jay Street, Bklyn	2	643-4900
Queensborough Community	56th Av/Springfield, Q	30	631-6262
College Mount St Vincent	Riverside & 263rd Street, Bx	19	*549-8000
College S.I. St George CUNY	130 Stuyvesant Place, S.I.	17	390-7951
College S.I. Sunnyside CUNY	715 Ocean Terrace, S.I.	15	390-7733
Downstate Medical SUNY	450 Clarkson Ave, Bklyn	11	270-1000
Einstein Med Coll (Yeshiva U)	1975 Eastchester Ave Bx	24	*430-2000
Fordham University	E Fordham & 3rd Ave, Bx	22	*579-2000
Herbert Lehman College CUNY	Bedford Pk Blvd W, Bx	21	*960-8000
Law School Queens College	200-01 42nd Street, Q	31	520-7000
Long Island University	University Plaza, Bklyn	6	834-6000
Manhattan College	Parkway & W 242nd St, Bx	20	*920-0100
NY Maritime College SUNY	Fort Schuyler, Bronx	26	*409-7200
NYC Technical College CUNY	300 Jay Street, Bklyn	2	643-4900
Polytechnic Institute NY	333 Jay Street, Bklyn	2	643-5000
Pratt Institute	200 Willoughby Ave, Bklyn	8	636-3600
Queens College CUNY	65-30 Kissena, Forst Hls, Q	31	520-7000
St. Francis College	180 Remsen Street, Bklyn	3	522-2300
St. John's University	Grand Centrl/Utopia Pkwy, Q	32	990-6161
St. Joseph's College	245 Clinton Avenue, Bklyn	9	636-6800
Wagner College	631 Howard Avenue, S.I.	16	390-3100
York College CUNY	150-14 Jamaica Avenue, Q	33	262-2000

MANHATTAN COLLEGES PAGE 64

*(Area 212)

ART TREASURES—OUTDOORS

Artist	Work of Art	Map No.	Map Page
Albers, Joseph	"Homage to the Square" lobby Pan Am	23	73
Bartholdi, Frederick A.	"Statue of Liberty"	36	58
Benton, Thomas Hart	Murals at the New School	30	64
Bitter, Karl	"Abundance" facade Pulitzer Fountain	2	8
Brown, Henry Kirke	"Washington" and "Lincoln" Union Sq	★	70
Calder, Alexander	"Guichet" stabile at Lincoln Center Library	★	56
Calder, Alexander	Stabile at U.S. Mission to UN	★	69
Calder, Alexander	"Three Red Wings" at World Trade Center	35	73
Carrere & Hustings	"Pulitzer Fountain"	2	8
Chagall, Marc	Murals at Metropolitan Opera	★	56
Chagall, Marc	Windows at the United Nations	★	69
Coutan, Jules	Clock sculpture facade of Grand Central	★	79
Dattner, Richard	Adventure Playground Central Pk at 65th	★	71
De Creeft, Jose	"Alice in Wonderland" Central Pk at 104th	★	71
Doyle, Alexander	"Horace Greeley" Greeley Sq, B'way & 34th		
Dubuffet, Jean	"Group of Four Trees" Chase Manhattan	39	73
Duncan, John	Grant's Tomb on Riverside Drive & 122nd	★	12
French, Daniel C.	"Alma Mater" Columbia	8	64
French, Daniel C.	"Four Figures" Custom House	F-2	76
Glaner, Fritz	Mural at Hammarskjold Library	★	69
Gottlieb, Adolph	"Glass Wall" Park Ave Synagogue	9	54
Gummer, Don	Hammarskjold Plaza Sculpture Garden	★	69
Hadzi, Dmitri	"The Hunt" sculpture at Avery Fisher Hall	★	56
Hepworth, Barbara	"Single Form" sculpture UN Courtyard	★	69
Hofman, Hans	Mosaic mural Third Ave betw 38 & 39 Sts		
Johnson, Philip	"Lincoln Center fountain"	★	56
Koening, Fritz	"Globe" World Trade Center	35	73
La Rue Johnson, Daniel	"Peace Form One" 50-ft obelisk at UN	★	69
Lawrie, Lee	"Atlas" Rockefeller Center	27	66
Leger, Fernand	Murals at UN General Assembly	★	69
Lippold, Richard	"Orpheus & Apollo" sculpture Avery Fisher	★	56
Lipton, Seymour	"Archangel" sculpture Avery Fisher Hall	★	56
Lober, Georg	"Hans Christian Andersen" Central Pk 74th	★	71
Manship, Paul	"Prometheus" at Ice Skating Rink	27	66
McComb, John Jr.	"Castle Clinton" at Battery Park	G-2	76
Moore, Henry	"Reclining Figure" in Reflecting Pool	★	56
Nevelson, Louise	"Night Presence IV" sculpture Park Ave & 92		
Nevelson, Louise	"Sculpture" at Juilliard School	★	56
Noguchi, Isamu	"Cube" Marine Midland Bank	38	73
Noguchi, Isamu	"Sunken Garden" Chase Manhattan	39	73
Picasso, Pablo	"Le Tricorne" at Seagram Bldg, Park & 52nd		
Picasso, Pablo	"Portrait of Sylvette" NYU Pei Plaza	33	64
Potter, E. C.	"Lions" Main Branch NYC Library	★	53
Rosati, James	"Steel Sculpture" World Trade Center	35	73
Rosenthal, Bernard	"Alamo" at Astor Place	3	8
Saint-Gaudens, Augustus	"General Sherman" Grand Army Plaza	2	8
Saint-Gaudens, Augustus	"Peter Cooper" at Cooper Square	F-2	40
Seth, Thomas	Clock on Fifth Ave between 43rd & 44th		
Smith, David	Sculpture in lobby of Vivian Beaumont	★	56
Stebbins, Emma	"Angel of the Waters" Central Pk at 72nd	★	71
Stoughton & Stoughton	"Soldiers & Sailors Memorial"	★	58
Ward, John Q. Adams	"Washington" Federal Hall Memorial	6	8
White, Stanford	"Washington Square Arch"	E-3	40
Museum of Modern Art Garden—designed by Philip Johnson		22	58

Sculptures by: Alexander Calder · Gaston Lachaise · Jacques Lipchitz · Henri Matisse · Henry Moore · Eli Nadelman · Pablo Picasso · David Smith · Pierre Auguste Renoir · Auguste Rodin

★ *Labeled on map*

ARCHITECTURAL LANDMARKS—ALPHABETICAL

Building	Architect	Date	Map Page	Map No.
Amer Mus Natural History	John Russell Pope	1936	58	**14**
Amer Tel & Telegraph	Welles Bosworth	1917	76	**E-2**
Association of the Bar	Cyrus L. W. Eidlitz	1895	42 W	44
Audubon Terrace	Charles P. Huntington	1908	58	★
Avery Fisher Hall	Max Abramowitz	1962	56	★
Bayard-Condict	Louis H. Sullivan	1898	40	**D-2**
Bowery Savings	York & Sawyer	1923	110 E	42
Brooklyn Bridge	John A. Roebling	1883	76	**E-4**
Carnegie Hall	Tuthill, Adler & Hunt	1891	57	**9**
Cath St. John the Divine	Heins & La Farge	1892+	54	**7**
Chanin	Sloan & Robertson	1929	73	**28**
Chase Manhattan Plaza	Skidmore Owings & Merrill	1960	76	**E-2**
Chrysler	William Van Alen	1929	73	**26**
Citicorp Center	H. Stubbins & E. Roth	1977	73	**8**
City Hall	Mangin McComb	1811	76	**D-2**
Colonnade Row	Alexander Jackson Davis	1838	40	**F-3**
Cooper Union Hall	Frederick A. Peterson	1859	40	**F-2**
Dakota Apartments	Henry J. Hardenbergh	1884	1 W 72nd	
Empire State	Shreve Lamb Harmon	1931	73	**30**
Federal Reserve Bank	York & Sawyer	1924	76	**E-2**
Flatiron	Daniel H. Burnham	1902	B'way & 23	
Ford Foundation	Roche & Dinkeloo	1967	320 E 43	
General Motors	Edward Stone & E. Roth	1968	73	**2**
Geo Washington Bridge	Cass Gilbert & O.H. Ammann	1931	8	★
Grace Church	James Renwick, Jr	1843	54	**49**
Grand Central Terminal	Warren Wetmore Reed Stem	1920	79	★
Guggenheim Museum	Frank Lloyd Wright	1959	58	**11**
Haughwout	John P. Gaynor	1856	76	**B-3**
Huntington Hartford	Edward Durell Stone	1964	200 W 58	
Juilliard School Music	Pietro Belluschi	1968	56	★
Lever House	Skidmore Owings & Merrill	1952	390 Park	
Low Memorial Library	McKim Mead & White	1897	64	**8**
Metropolitan Museum Art	Richard Morris Hunt	1890	58	**12**
Metropolitan Opera House	Wallace K. Harrison	1966	56	★
Morgan Library	McKim Mead & White	1901	58	**26**
N.Y. Historical Society	York & Sawyer	1908	58	**15**
N.Y. Public Library	Carrere & Hustings	1911	53	★
N.Y. State Theater	Philip C. Johnson	1964	56	★
N.Y. Stock Exchange	George B. Post	1903	76	**F-2**
N.Y. Telephone Hdqtrs	Ralph T. Walker	1917	76	**E-2**
Old Merchant's House	Minard Lafeber	1800	29 E 4th	
Pan Am	Walter Gropius	1963	73	**23**
R. C. A.	Raymond Hood	1933	73	**15**
Riverside Church	Ralph Cram & Chas Collens	1930	54	**3**
St. Patrick's Cathedral	James Renwick, Jr.	1879	54	**31**
St. Paul's Church	Thomas McBean	1766	54	**27**
Seagram	Mies van der Rohe	1958	Park & 52	
Temple Emanu-el	Clarence S. Stein	1929	54	**23**
Trinity Church	Richard Upjohn	1846	76	**F-2**
United Nations	Wallace K. Harrison	1952	69	★
U.S. Customs House	Cass Gilbert	1907	76	**F-2**
Villard Houses	McKim Mead & White	1886	Mad & 50	
Vivian Beaumont Theater	Eero Saarinen	1965	56	★
Whitney Museum of Art	M. Breuer & H. Smith	1966	58	**16**
Woolworth	Cass Gilbert	1913	73	**34**
World Trade Center	Yamasaki & Roth	1974	73	**35**

★ Labelled on Map

NEW YORK TREASURES

Museums and Institutions are located by Map No. and Page

	Map No	Map Page
ANCIENT CULTURES		
Asia · Rockefeller collection; Pan-Asian from earliest to 19th century	19	59
Egyptian · 40,000 artifacts · largest collection outside Cairo	12	59
Egyptian & Classical Art · sculpture, friezes textiles from 5 millenia	8	82
Indians · No./Cent./So. Amer. · Aborigine cultures, pre-historic to date	3	59
Primitive Art · Rockefeller's: 15,000 items fr Africa, Americas, Pacific	12	59
BOOKS & MANUSCRIPTS		
Art Books · over 80,000 books and periodicals	22	59
Black Culture · 75,000 vols, 50,000 photos, music, Afro-Amer artifacts	4	59
Guttenberg Bibles · & Medieval, Renaissance illuminated manuscripts	26	59
Hispanic · 102,000 volumes, also paintings, murals, artifacts	3	59
Judaica · most extensive collection of artifacts in the world	8	59
Presidential Papers · 2,500 historical documents and memorabilia	29	59
Rare Books · 91,000 volumes including Guttenberg Bible, first folio Shakespeare, Bay Psalm bk 1640, Christopher Columbus' letter 1493	MAIN LIB	53
FURNITURE & DECORATIVE ARTS		
American · period rooms, paintings · Colonial thru the 20th century	12	59
Designs · over 30,000: theater, furniture, textile, ceramic, ornaments...	9	59
Faberge · 200 *objets de luxe* including 10 Russian Easter Eggs	29	59
Tiffany Collection · over 200 items · lamps, windows, *objets d'art*	15	59
NATURAL SCIENCES		
Bronx Zoo · 262 acres, 3,600 animals, 700 species, World of Darkness · day/nite reversal; World of Birds · Jungle World, reptiles	32	82
Gems · 21,000 carat topaz, 563 carat sapphire, 100 carat star ruby...	14	59
Gardens · 50 acres, 13,000 species of plants, 13 specialized gardens	9	82
Haupt Conservatory · Victorian glass palace with 11 environments	29	82
Marine Life · 20,000 specimens of over 225 species; 4 Beluga whales	14	82
25 Million Artifacts · dinosaurs, primates, whales, mammals, birds	14	59
PAINTINGS & SCULPTURE		
American Contemporary · complete collection also Calder's "Circus"	16	59
Audubon · 433 original watercolors depicting birds of North America	15	59
Drawings · Renaissance · 19th century, Michaelangelo, Rembrandt...	26	59
European · 14th to 18th century Masters, world renowned collection	12	59
European · paintings, furniture, tapestries in 14th-19th century setting	17	59
Impressionist · largest collection outside of France	12	59
Medieval · 8th to 16th cen Gothic & Romanesque art and architecture; part of 4 cloisters; a chapel, 12th cen apse, unicorn tapestries	1	59
Modern · 100,000 paintings, sculpture, drawings · 1880 to present	22	59
Non Objective Art · International collection including Brancusi's "Muse"; viewed from Frank Lloyd Wright's spiraling ramp	11	59
MISCELLANEOUS		
Costumes · worldwide collection 17th cen to present couturier fashions	12	59
Film Collection · 8,000 films and over 3 million stills, also screenings	22	59
Maps · over 370,000 maps of the world from the beginning of time	LABEL	53
Miniature Models · 12,000 toy soldiers in 'action' · 500 crafts & ships	29	59
New York Panorama · 9,000 sq ft model, 855,000 bldgs (1" equals 100')	43	82
Richmondtown Restoration · 96 acres, 30 historic bldgs, 17-19th cen	23	83
Statue of Liberty · 1886 gift of France, restored by 2.5 million donations	36	59

See pages 84-85 for Architectural Landmarks and Outdoor Statuary

SUBURBS & METROPOLITAN AREA COMMUNITIES

Community	1980 census	Approx *miles	Community	1980 census	Approx *miles
WESTCHESTER COUNTY — NEW YORK					
Bedford	15,137	40	New Rochelle	70,794	18
Briarcliff	7,115	30	Ossining	20,196	35
Bronxville	6,267	17	Rye	15,083	26
Chappaqua	15,425	35	Scarsdale	17,650	21
Harrison	23,046	26	Tarrytown	10,648	18
Mamaroneck	17,616	20	White Plains	46,999	25
Mt. Kisco	8,025	39	Yonkers	195,351	14
Mt. Vernon	66,713	16	Yorktown	31,988	40
NASSAU · SUFFOLK COUNTIES — NEW YORK					
Amityville	9,076	39	Levittown	57,045	27
Babylon	12,388	45	Lindenhurst	26,919	41
Bay Shore	10,784	50	Long Beach	34,073	27
Bethpage	16,840	33	Lynbrook	20,424	22
Commack	34,719	44	Manhasset	8,485	18
Copiague	20,132	40	Massapequa	19,779	36
East Meadow	39,317	26	Merrick	24,478	29
Farmingdale	7,946	60	Mineola	20,757	26
Floral Park	16,805	20	New Hyde Pk	9,801	24
Freeport	38,272	28	Oyster Bay	6,497	35
Garden City	22,927	23	Port Washington	14,521	23
Glen Cove	24,618	25	Rockville Centre	25,412	24
Great Neck	9,168	20	Roslyn Heights	6,546	23
Hempstead	40,404	22	Syosset	9,818	32
Hicksville	43,245	31	Valley Stream	35,769	22
Huntington	21,727	37	Wantagh	19,817	32
Islip	13,438	52	Westbury	13,871	26
FAIRFIELD COUNTY — CONNECTICUT					
Bridgeport	142,546	61	New Canaan	17,931	44
Darien	18,892	39	Norwalk	77,767	43
Fairfield	54,849	56	Stamford	102,453	35
Greenwich	59,578	31	Westport	25,290	46
BERGEN COUNTY — NEW JERSEY					
Bergenfield	25,568	14	Lodi	23,956	14
Cliffside Park	21,464	6	Palisades Pk	13,732	11
Dumont	18,334	15	Paramus	26,474	16
Englewood	23,701	9	Ridgefield (area)	23,032	12
Fair Lawn	32,229	20	Rutherford	19,608	9
Fort Lee	32,449	7	Teaneck	39,007	11
Hackensack	36,039	14	Tenafly	13,552	14
HUDSON · ESSEX · MORRIS COUNTIES — NEW JERSEY					
Bayonne	64,047	10	Lyndhurst	20,326	10
Bloomfield	47,792	13	Madison	15,357	29
Clifton	74,388	13	Maplewood	22,950	18
E Orange	77,690	17	Montclair	38,321	15
Hoboken	42,460	4	Morristown	16,614	33
Irvington	61,493	16	Newark	329,248	12
Jersey City	223,532	5	No. Bergen	47,019	5
Kearny	35,735	15	Union City	50,184	4
UNION · MIDDLESEX COUNTIES — NEW JERSEY					
Elizabeth	106,201	17	Springfield	13,955	22
Linden	37,836	21	Summit	21,071	26
Rahway	26,723	24	Westfield	30,447	26
Roselle	20,641	22	Woodbridge	90,074	27

*To midtown NYC-(Because of the many routes into the city, mileages may vary.)

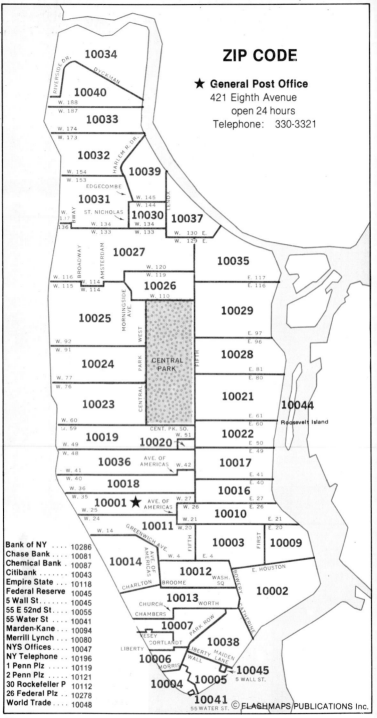

ZIP CODE

★ **General Post Office**
421 Eighth Avenue
open 24 hours
Telephone: 330-3321

10034
10040
W. 188
W. 187
10033
W. 174
W. 173
10032
RIVERSIDE DR.
DYCKMAN
HARLEM R. DR.
10039
W. 154
W. 153
EDGECOMBE
W. 145
10031
W. 144
ST. NICHOLAS
LENOX
W. 17
B'WAY
10030
10037
136
W. 134
W. 134
W. 133
W. 133
W. 130 E.
W. 129 E.
10027
BROADWAY
AMSTERDAM
W. 120
W. 119
10035
E. 117
W. 116
W. 115
W. 114
W. 114
10026
E. 116
10029
W. 110
MORNINGSIDE AVE.
10025
WEST
E. 97
E. 96
10028
CENTRAL PARK
FIFTH
W. 92
W. 91
W. 77
W. 76
10024
E. 81
E. 80
CENTRAL PARK
10023
10021
W. 60
W. 59
CENT. PK. SO.
E. 61
E. 60
10044
Roosevelt Island
10019
10020
W. 51
10022
E. 50
E. 49
W. 49
W. 48
10036
AVE. OF AMERICAS
W. 42
10017
E. 41
E. 40
W. 41
W. 40
10018
W. 36
W. 35
10016
E. 27
E. 26
10001 ★
AVE. OF AMERICAS
W. 27
W. 26
10010
W. 25
W. 24
10011
W. 21
E. 21
E. 20
FIFTH
FIRST
W. 14
GREENWICH AVE.
10003
10009
AVE. OF AMERICAS
W. 4
E. 4
10014
E. HOUSTON
10012
WASH. SQ.
BROOME
CHARLTON
BOWERY
CATHERINE
10002
CHURCH
10013
WORTH
CHAMBERS
PARK ROW
10007
VESEY
CORTLANDT
10038
LIBERTY
10006
LIBERTY
MAIDEN LANE
WALL
MORRIS
10045
5 WALL ST.
10005
10004
10041
55 WATER ST.
© FLASHMAPS PUBLICATIONS Inc.

Bank of NY 10286
Chase Bank 10081
Chemical Bank . 10087
Citibank 10043
Empire State .. 10118
Federal Reserve 10045
5 Wall St....... 10045
55 E 52nd St... 10055
55 Water St 10041
Marden-Kane .. 10094
Merrill Lynch .. 10080
NYS Offices 10047
NY Telephone .. 10196
1 Penn Plz 10119
2 Penn Plz 10121
30 Rockefeller P 10112
26 Federal Plz .. 10278
World Trade 10048